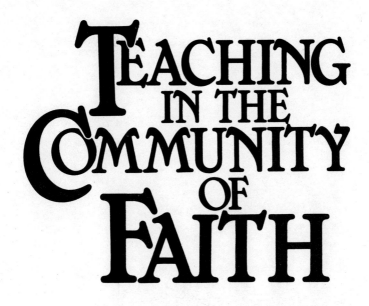

TEACHING
IN THE
COMMUNITY
OF
FAITH

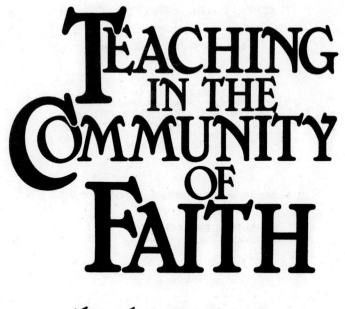

TEACHING
IN THE
COMMUNITY
OF
FAITH

Charles R. Foster

105364

Abingdon Press
Nashville

TEACHING IN THE COMMUNITY OF FAITH

Library of Congress Cataloging in Publication Data

FOSTER, CHARLES R., 1937–
    Teaching in the community of faith.
    1. Christian education—Philosophy.
    I. Title.
    BV1464.F67   207   82-6641   AACR2

ISBN 0-687-41086-X

MANUFACTURED BY THE PARTHENON PRESS AT
NASHVILLE, TENNESSEE, UNITED STATES OF AMERICA

I dedicate this book to four of my significant teachers: Anne and Scott, who have taught me to see and hear again with the eyes and ears of children; Frank B. Wyatt, my grandfather and pastor to many; and Thomas M. Steen, a colleague in ministry, whose clarity of vision, freedom of spirit, and depth of commitment have revealed to me the power of childlike faith.

CONTENTS

FOREWORD

In 1960, J. Stanley Glen called for the "recovery of the teaching ministry" in a little book with that title.[1] Two decades later, many of the issues that had caught his attention are still alive in much of American Protestantism—the area of church life I know best. The biblical message continues to be domesticated and used in all-too-simplistic fashion. It remains strangely silent in the deliberations over ethical, political, and economic problems faced by contemporary women and men in both personal realm and public world. The excitement and immediate gratification of experiential religion still contribute to the avoidance of what Glen described as the "offensive" character of the gospel. Clergy continue to abdicate their responsibilities to teach. Laity continue to see themselves implementing an educational program, as instructional technicians, rather than as mediators of the grace and truth of God's ever creative and redemptive Word. The educational programs of our congregations all too often produce passive disciples—laity who cannot look at the events of their lives with theological or ethical categories to illumine their experience, who all too often engage in self-serving outreach and mission activities, and who lack even the basic skills and resources to participate in the liturgy of the congregation with meaning and power.

For Glen, reclaiming the teaching function in the church was necessary in order to hold together the "intelligible," or cognitive, and "noumenal," or experiential, content of the church's faith.[2] He keenly sensed the pervasive subordination of teaching to experience in the church. While that issue is no less critical today, the urgency behind my own quest for the recovery of the teaching ministry comes from a somewhat different source.

It has to do primarily with the relationship of the Christian educator to the world in which we live. Since Horace Bushnell wrote his tract on Christian nurture in 1847, most interpreters of Protestant church education have approached their task from the vantage point of their own participation in an expanding political, economic, and religious milieu. They represented the general values and perspectives of those people and groups shaping our national, as well as religious, future, even when they disagreed over specific programs or issues. They viewed their task as being participants in a majority consciousness within our national life.

The result may be seen in the optimism of Christian educators who envisioned a world of harmony and peace emerging, in part, through the programmatic emphases of the institutional church, and who assumed a social context for church education marked by stability, security, continuity, and progress. In a very real sense, this approach to Christian education has been informed significantly by what Walter Brueggeman has called "a theology of management and celebration."[3] Both the thought and the structures of contemporary church education have emerged in a political and religious climate of relative security and well-being. Our major struggles during the past several decades, while very real, have essentially been debates among ourselves over theological or educational presuppositions. Most of our energy, however, has been spent on issues relating to the direction and management of our ever expanding and diversifying programs. Any seminary or church library will illustrate this fact. Most of the books in the field focus on ways to strengthen the local church's educational ministry. Even the few major theoreticians writing in the field have assumed that the existing institutional framework for the church's educational ministry will be the primary vehicle for building up the body of Christ in the future.

I do not now intend to criticize or call into question this predominant approach to interpretations of church education in American Protestantism. Brueggeman has already pointed out that this perspective is important. It reflects the experience and situation of the "haves" in society—from ancient Israel to the present—who in times of prosperity and peace have brought order and stability to the life of the people. Their contribution has been significant. "It is the well-off," Bruggeman observes, "who can reflect on proper management, who are aware that blessings have been given to them that must be wisely cared for and properly maintained for the generations to come. It is the well-off who can be reflective enough to care intentionally about the joyous celebration of life."[4] They have helped us to know and to appreciate the beauty, the order, and the harmony revealed in creation.

The signs of our being among the "haves" of the world are certainly around us. Our economic wealth (both national and ecclesiastical), our military might, our ability to play vast political games, our capacity to respond to major human crises with expansive gifts of food, medical supplies, and other resources, perpetuate the image we have of ourselves as a blessed nation.

Our well-being, however, is increasingly threatened. Recent national events have demonstrated that our words and our actions are not readily accepted as persuasive by many around the world. We have been humbled by our inability to effect peace in Viet Nam and the Middle East. We have been humiliated in Iran. We have been impotent in the new economic games, played first by OPEC and now by other groups of nations. We have been unable to persuade many of our "allies" to cooperate with us in sanctions against other governments, to promote what we have determined to be the common good for the world. We increasingly find ourselves standing alone in votes in the United Nations. We are still a powerful and dominant nation, but increasingly we find ourselves having to negotiate our concerns from a position of being "one among many," rather than "one before many." All these experiences challenge the security of our national self-understanding and undermine our sense of well-being. They are a threat to our national identity.

It is not my intention to discuss the relationship of the "haves" and "have nots" among the nations of the world, although that discussion is relevant to the way we view ourselves as the church in that social environment. Rather, my specific concern is with the way we respond to the increasing loss of status and place of the Christian community in our larger society. In spite of large church membership and much media attention to some Christian perspectives, our experience is increasingly that of a people no longer in charge. Clergy no longer have the political clout they once enjoyed in many sectors of our national life. Our ethical impulses have been reduced (all too often, in recent years, by active church people), to simplistic and moralistic platitudes in many contemporary social, political, and economic controversies. Many of our symbols, appropriated by the adherents of what is often called our national "civil religion," have lost their hold on our personal and corporate imagination. Our rituals have been trivialized, and the stories of our heritage have been called sentimental and irrelevant. The blessings of our common heritage and life, in other words, often seem superficial and lifeless.

At the same time, the influence of the church in the public sector is also decreasing. As I am writing these words, local church leaders and pastors in the community I live in are now facing the fact that the schools of the community can no longer act as extensions of a Protestant subculture. Students come from many religious backgrounds—Jewish, Hindu, Muslim, Ba-hai, and Buddhist, as well as Christian. The church people in this town, however, have difficulty imagining a future that is truly inclusive of all religious traditions without being, at the same time, essentially Protestant Christian. Their dilemma?

Ours? We do not know how to live as one among many. We do not know how to think of ministry and mission from the vantage point of being a minority people.

Perhaps our experience has some similarities to that of the Jews in Babylon. Removed from their homes and taken to a distant land, they were surrounded by a majority who did not share their history, were not interested in their vision of the future, and did not appreciate the rituals and symbols that nurtured their common life. As Christians in the latter decades of the twentieth century, we find ourselves experiencing a similar dislocation. We may not have moved from our homes, but we, too, find ourselves increasingly aware of the presence of the majority of people around the world who express little interest in our view of the future and do not appreciate our rituals and symbols. Just as the Babylonian exiles had to learn to live in a new way, so we in our own psychological exile must perceive and organize our experience in relation to our emerging status in the world. As Brueggeman points out, our faith tradition has rich resources for such a task. Rooted in what he calls a "theology of survival,"[5] the exodus and exile provide images to guide the work of Christian educators that are alternatives to those images of dominance found in a "theology of management."

The task of learning to live in, and relate to, our world in a new way will not be easy. Perhaps this fact is most evident in the casual way our churches approach the task of transmitting to the next generation the values, commitments, and practices we hold most dear. We continue to use school models designed to socialize a minority population into the majority. We subordinate the teaching function in our churches to the nurture of positive human relations, or subvert it in procedures through which students acquire biblical and doctrinal information unrelated to the ethical issues of their and our lives. We seem to be deliberately fostering yet another generation of biblically illiterate, theologically inept, and ethically shallow persons. Such people will not be prepared to keep alive the promises of the covenant of our spiritual ancestors as we dwell in an increasingly alien land in an increasingly fragmented world. When self-conscious people with a keen sense of their corporate identity and a commitment to the future acknowledge their participation in a pluralistic world, they do not assume that their values and commitments will be naturally handed on to subsequent generations, or that existing educational structures and resources will work. Rather, I believe, they take the processes of transmission (including teaching) most seriously.

This essay, consequently, gathers up and orders some of the central themes in my own quest to recover a sense of the church's responsibility to teach those who would call themselves disciples of Jesus Christ in this day and in our contemporary situation. The focus of this work will not be on what teachers do. There are already many books and resources available that describe how teachers may plan for and carry out their classroom responsibilities. Rather, I intend to explore what teaching does in, and for, the good of a people with a common history and a shared vision of the future. St. Paul claimed that teaching was a gift to the church for the sake of building it up as the body of Christ. Teaching is crucial in any community concerned with its own destiny. It is an essential function of any community concerned with being faithful to its heritage and responsible for its future. Hence, my starting point is naturally with an exploration of the meaning of community, especially that community of faith identified with Abraham and Sarah, Moses and the prophets, and designated as the contemporary embodiment of the commitments of Jesus Christ and his early followers.

Within that framework, the second chapter will explore one specific dimension of the God-human relationship as developed in the biblical literature. The image of the community as "children of God" was selected not only because contemporary church educators, along with their counterparts in public education, tend to be more fascinated with the differences than with the similarities among children, youth, and adults; but even more, because it may help us approach a view of teaching that is not inherently hierarchical.

This theme is picked up again in the third chapter, which reverses the way we often look at the goals of church education. Rather than taking our paradigm for faithfulness from the character of adulthood, the admonition of Jesus to be faithful like a child seems somehow particularly appropriate for those of us in the church today. This chapter will focus on the characteristics of faithfulness to be found in childlikeness.

The final chapter explores the nature and function of teaching as an activity of any self-conscious community concerned with introducing new generations into its common life and vision for the future. Attention will be focused on the functions and tasks embodied in what teaching does for the building up of the community, and the characteristics of those who become the teachers for the community.

This quest has been a challenging one in which many people have shared. I am especially appreciative of the contributions of students, local church pastors, directors of Christian education, and church school teachers in classes, seminars, and workshops, for sharing in my own struggles with the issues and ideas discussed in subsequent pages. I am grateful, moreover, for the critical suggestions and comments of several of my colleagues and friends on the faculty at the Methodist Theological School in Ohio and in several nearby parishes. Their unwavering support and encouragement certainly have helped me to bring this project to completion. Sharon Ringe, Everett Tilson, and Robert Browning; along with Dale Hindmarsh, Edward Trimmer, and Ronald Payne deserve special mention. My wife, Janet, and our children, Anne and Scott, have been consistent sources of new insight as I have sought to understand more fully the meaning of living in community. And last, but far from least, I appreciate the ever-cheerful support of the faculty secretaries at Methesco and Scarritt; Sharon Creasy, Barbara Anderson, and Kay Carter.

CHAPTER 1

CHILDREN
OF GOD
Members of a Community

Then God said, "And now we will make human beings;
They will be like us and resemble us."

So God created human beings, making them to be
like himself. He created them male and female, blessed
them, and said, "Have many children, so that your
descendents will live all over the earth and bring it
under your control."

God looked at everything He had made, and He was
very pleased.   (Gen. 1:26a, 27-28a, 31a, GNB)

Our Commonality Is in Community

People are, first and foremost, children—children of God.
This biblical perspective means, as Walter Brueggeman has
written, that "all persons are children of a single family,
members of a single tribe, heirs of a single hope, and bearers of
a single destiny."[1] For Brueggeman, this claim is rooted in the
most basic of all biblical visions: "that all of creation is one,
every creature in community with every other, living in
harmony and security toward the joy and well-being of every
other creature."[2] Indeed, when we begin with the affirmation
that for the Old Testament Hebrew, Abraham is the father of
all Israel; and the New Testament affirmation that in Jesus
Christ our unity is found in our obeisance to his lordship, we

acknowledge that we are bound together in a common loyalty with a shared status not unlike that held by children.

The same point is made in a different way by John Sutcliffe. "It is of the nature of the church to be inclusive rather than exclusive." If we begin with this affirmation, it is consequently inconceivable to proclaim a God of love on the one hand, and on the other hand to erect barriers that "exclude some on the grounds of age, education or their ability to express their commitment in the formal language of the church."[3] Whether we begin with the recognition of the commonality of our status as the children of creation or of our interdependence as members of the body of Christ, we are led to view children as no more, and no less, the children of God than the adults who care for them.

This perspective permeates the biblical record. In the Genesis creation narrative, the writer claims that *we have a common ancestry*—no matter what our race, culture, or age. Consequently we may each claim that we are descendents of the original and archetypal man and woman of creation. In the process we each share the stamp of God's approval on our very existence. We are born with the image of God impressed upon our very being. We are made to bear the likeness of God. We do not have to search for the characteristics of given ancestors in the face or temperament of a child, as grandparents often do, to discern the God-likeness in each person. It is a stamp we all bear—no matter what lines of social, economic, racial, cultural, sexual, or national barriers we may set up to disguise that fact.

Again no matter what our age or condition *we have a common heritage as well.* As the followers of Jesus Christ, we claim with St. Paul, that Abraham and Sarah are our spiritual parents. Nowhere is this relationship more poignantly evoked than in the spiritual, "Rock-a My Soul in the Bosom of Abraham." In the singing of this song, we acknowledge that we are gathered into and under the identity of a man whose faith in God, along with that of Sarah, has helped shape people's faith into the present moment. Metaphorically, we are the fruits of their seed scattered down through the ages and throughout the lands of the earth. In our faithfulness to the God of Abraham and Sarah, we witness to the steadfastness of the faithfulness of God to them. We are gathered up into a faithful relationship that is so high it cannot be transcended, so deep it cannot be avoided, and so wide that it cannot be escaped.

And in a third way, the biblical narrative reveals that no matter what our age or station in life, *we also have a common experience.* The people of Israel were often called the children of God.[4] From such a perspective, we are each sons and daughters of the One who created and sustains us—a relationship that anticipates the intimacy of the family but is not bound by our nuclear representations of that historic form of social organization.

To claim that each of us is a child of God—no matter what our age—has radical consequences. It reminds us that the distance in maturity, wisdom, age, perspective, or ability between the young child and the older adult is small indeed, when contrasted with the chasm that exists in any comparison between God and ourselves. Indeed, it is ironic to claim for ourselves a status, a position, a power and authority that exceed that used to describe Jesus the Christ, our Lord and Redeemer. For if he is to be called the Son of God, it is audacious to claim for ourselves any relationship that claims a higher status or authority. We are no more and no less than creations—children, if you will—of God.

Hence I begin our inquiry into the church's teaching ministry with a faith statement: "In the beginning, God . . . ." It provides the springboard, as well as the goal and framework, for our explorations. It alters the perspective that informs most contemporary discussions on education. Instead of being fascinated initially with the uniqueness of each person, I have been impressed by the common threads that permeate the human community. Instead of looking upon society as an aggregate of individuals, I perceive each person as a necessary part of the social milieu. Themes of interdependence rather than independence dominate my attention. *Community* takes precedence as a category for understanding the nature and meaning of existence, rather than personal identity. This is not to conclude that our uniqueness, independence, and individuality are not important. Rather it is to take seriously Urban Holmes' description of the Hebraic view of the "corporate person," in which the "individual embodies the community, and the community is responsible for the individual." People in this definition are not discrete individuals, but are what they are "by virtue of" their "membership in the community."[5] One of the most powerful and formative of all human experiences, in other words, is to be found in our connectedness—our relatedness—with each other, with all of creation, and with God.

The "Community of Faith"

"We live by images," Robert McAfee Brown has observed, because they are "suggestive rather than exhaustive. They trigger responses that go beyond what they visually and verbally convey."[6] It is precisely for this reason that I have chosen to employ the image of the *community of faith*, both to guide and to set the frame for our look at the nature and function of teaching in the church. I do so in spite of the ambiguity that often surrounds our use of the word *community*. In this case I am not employing the image as "a definable, quantifiable entity that can be created and sustained by a corporate act of will, based on a location and a task."[7] This common approach tends to dominate both much of the research in the social sciences and also the perspective of people in general.[8] *Community,* as I intend to use it, will connote neither "turf," (place), nor "task" (a given institutional structure and program), to use the succinct terms employed by Robert Evans.[9]

Rather, it is my intention to allow the image *community of faith* to function symbolically for us. At this point I am following the seminal work of Carl Jung, Paul Tillich, and Louis Sherrill. Their explication of the nature and function of symbols is most helpful. Sherrill, for example, has defined *symbol* as a sign representing that "to which it points, not because it has been arbitrarily chosen for that purpose, but because it is intrinsically related to it in some way, such as by association with it, or participation in it."[10]

In illustrating the relation of a symbol to the reality it points to or participates in, Sherrill used a schema looking like an inverted "A."[11] For reasons that may appear obvious later, I prefer to reverse his depiction of the way a symbol functions for us.

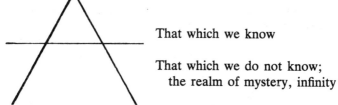

That which we know

That which we do not know; the realm of mystery, infinity

The small triangle at the top represents our experience of the reality caught up in the whole figure. It is the part we can see, hear, touch, or taste. It is that segment of which we are conscious. But it is only a small part of the reality. Indeed, the two outside lines could be drawn into infinity. What we "know" is consequently a very small part of the reality indeed. Such is the case when we use the word-symbol "God." What we know about God, or the God we know, is only a small part of the totality of what we can know. And yet, even this small amount of knowledge is enough for us to order our lives around it.

Similarly, the cross functions for Christians as a symbol, because two crossed boards both point to and participate in a reality much more vast and incomprehensible than the immediate realities of an instrument of torture and death can convey. It effectively gathers up the power of such very human experiences as sacrifice, forgiveness, and redemption, and yet it transcends them by opening up to us ever deeper meanings in those same experiences. That greater power functions as a springboard for many of the deeper commitments and meanings that give our lives purpose and direction.

The image of the community of faith functions in a similar way. In the pages that follow, it is my intention to use that image as a symbolic description of *the gathered responses of people to the initiative of God, in which both our corporate identity as the body of Christ and our personal identities as his followers are revealed.* In other words, as people respond to God's initiative, they participate in the symbolic power evoked by the community of faith. As people ignore God's initiative, they contribute to the fragmentation of that historic fellowship of the faithful. As people respond to God's initiative, they discover the potential and power of personhood—the uniqueness of their own createdness. As they ignore God's initiative, they lose touch with their connectedness and consequently with the distinctiveness of their own createdness.

The "community of faith" image may function symbolically for us because it both points to, and participates in, one of the most powerful expressions of our relationship to God. It may be seen in our longing for communion or in our impetus to intimacy that dominates so many of our interactions with others. The power of the friendly gesture in evoking a responsive chord, the dread of isolation, or the fear of loneliness all point to the inherently human quest for community.

This quest is deeply embedded in the Christian life-stream. We long, as Evans has noted, for the immediacy and intensity of the relationships portrayed in the descriptions of the first gatherings of Christians in The Book of the Acts of the Apostles. The picture of a "whole body of believers . . . united in heart and soul" (Acts 4:32, NEB) projects a vision of fellowship and intimacy that so far exceeds our most significant experiences in our local congregations that we often feel cheated.[12] And yet the expectation that we, too, might share in the unity of that community is among the most powerful and compelling sources of the journey of faith for many in our churches today.

The vision of that experience of communion with others and with God is an elusive one for us. Robert Evans has observed that the experience many people have in their own congregations is so far from the ideal projected in Acts that "they either scoff at the ideal as an impossible dream, or respond to the unrealized theological interpretation of Acts with frustrated anger."[13] Such indignation, Evans suggests, "seldom vents itself in a constructive response." Anger rooted in frustration may expose a desire for community, which has erupted into hostility primarily because a basic human need has been thwarted. Evans agrees with Robert MacAfee Brown that this anger may reveal that we in the church have sold out on our own vision and have become, in the process, no more than a pale reflection of the world around us.[14] The intensity of these responses may reveal the power of the common quest for the kind of interrelatedness caught up in the image of the community of faith. It is rooted in our shared hunger to be connected with the source and product of the very act of creation itself.

Of course, another part of the same story of our origins has to do with the human desire to resist that same interrelatedness. We want to be "free"—to be able to sit outside our involvements and relationships to judge the manner and the extent of our participation with others. This perspective, Paul Minear reminds us, reduces our concept of the church to an "it." The experience of community we seek becomes, in the process, impersonal in character, and a "nebulous distance" emerges between "it" and ourselves.[15] The interrelatedness we seek consequently seems out of our reach. It remains noticeably removed from our inner quests. Only in rare moments, when caught up in some spontaneous and overwhelming event, do we experience the solidarity of the "we" of community we seek, rather than the distance of the community that functions as "it" in our lives. In the push and pull of our longing for being connected to the source of life and to the rest of creation and our resistance to being caught up in that same relationship, we often find ourselves angry for not experiencing what seems to be promised to us in various accounts in the Old and New Testaments. We feel cheated of the deeper meanings of existence. We find ourselves compelled to pursue that proverbial "carrot" of intimacy dangling in front of us.

At this point I wish to reiterate that the image "community of faith" can in no way embody the depth and breadth of its symbolic potential for us. Instead, just as my version of Sherrill's schema illustrates, it gathers up only a part of the reality in which we all participate. This reality is envisioned for us in some of the gatherings of those early Christians recorded in The Acts of the Apostles, but it functions as a vision or dream that cannot be reduced to words or pictures, structures or programs. Yet it compels us, often in the midst of our resistance, to continue the quest. And at the same time, it judges the inadequacy of our efforts to engage in the harmonious relationships intended in creation.

The "community of faith" has, for me, the potential to reveal something of what it means to be a part of the fellowship of the children of God. It reflects their experience down through the ages, as well as points to the meaning and power in that relationship in which people are bound to God and to each other in love, justice, hope, and peace—again, word-symbols inadequate to express our intended meanings. It is an image grounded in experience, but not confined by experience. It is encountered in the realms of our time and our space, but it is not bound by time and space. Consequently, I will use the phrase *community of faith* to describe the fellowship of those who call themselves Christian, with the expectation that we may discover in its deeper meanings the potential to illumine and transform the structures, relationships, and rituals to be found in the institutions and programs we create to receive and hand on the traditions and values of our common life.

The Initiative of God: The Source of a Community

Perhaps we who call ourselves Christian educators encounter no greater stumbling block in our own faith pilgrimages than in our tendency to act as if the so-called development of faith in those we teach is dependent upon us. The very steps involved in planning and conducting a teaching-learning experience may lull us into an easy ignorance of the sources and inspiration for our actions. The possession of information, concepts, and strategies not directly available to those we teach may blind us to the vast amount we do not know or will never understand. The patterns of dependence we so often foster in those we teach may well inhibit our awareness that we do not give them the impetus for learning.

Rather, the community of faith was, and continues to be, created by the initiative of God *in the responses* of people to a destiny not fully understood. Indeed, that faithfulness may develop in spite of our efforts to teach or lead. This seemingly contradictory statement may be illustrated by recalling the biblical record, in which God's initiative is repeatedly revealed in the responses of people. In other words, concrete actions by specific people and groups of people revealed to others the power of God to shape and direct their lives. Such actions are often caught up in our words "witnessing," "teaching," "prophesying," or "serving," but they involve a distinctive orientation that we often ignore. These actions have had formative power in the community because they embody the responses of people to the call of God.

Abraham and Sarah, for example, did not gather up their household, pack their bags, and undertake that strange, and undoubtedly often dangerous, journey toward a "promised land" to proclaim the good news of God's love or to teach their friends and relatives about the wondrous mystery of God's grace. Rather, they responded to a vision of a life encompassing a distinctive relationship with God. It took them to a strange land. It led them into some awesome predicaments. It confronted them with the shallowness of their faithfulness. It persisted in leading them onward. Risking the known for the unknown, they revealed in their living that they had been seized and redirected by God. Similarly, people down through the ages have participated in the continuing stream of faithful responding that we trace back to the faith of Abraham and Sarah.

We may remember the names of some of these great people of faith. Moses, Deborah, Joseph, David, Elijah, Isaiah, Esther, Dorcas, Paul, and the disciples emerge as people representative of the entire community, whose faithfulness has been nurtured by the responsiveness of others to the ever-present initiative of God in our lives. They serve as symbols of the corporate response of a people to the initiative of God's activity in such historical events as the Exodus, the forming of the nation of Israel, the Babylonian captivity, the Incarnation, and the organization of those small struggling congregations around the Mediterranean.

The adult character of our societies has all too often blinded us to the fact that God's actions are not confined only to those who have reached some form of socially determined maturity. Neither are the models of faithfulness to be found among adults alone. The biblical accounts are not numerous, but one cannot overlook Samuel's encounter, as a small boy, with the voice of God. The Incarnation occurred in the form of an infant. A young boy offered his lunch to the possibility that the crowd surrounding Jesus might be fed. Jesus called the children to come to him, and his teaching did not consist of a lengthy discourse; instead he touched them. He took them into his arms—a profound extension of the bond of community as anyone who has experienced the snuggling hug of a child would know. That act conveys the response of one who has been loved. It embodies a relational promise of great power.

Our responses, no matter how effective in revealing the love and power of God, can never be equated with the initiative of God. Instead, they simply provide us with a brief glimpse into the wondrous variety of ways God works in and through people calling those around them to lives of faith and obedience. We did not see the burning bush, but we have heard of the consequences of that encounter in the subsequent events of Moses' life and have seen it in people's responses to similar circumstances in our own time. Martin Luther King, among others, heard that same call to lead his people out of bondage—an ancient call, but a contemporary response. We did not hear the still, small voice, but we have been confronted by the persistence of Elijah's commitments in the face of overwhelming adversity. Perhaps Mother Theresa's persistent patience illustrates a similar pattern of faithfulness in the face of adversity. We will never be able to claim that we heard Jesus call those four fishermen to follow him, but we do know something of the impact of that event upon the course of the world even into the present moment. These glimpses (for they are no more than that) become both the content for our teaching and the signposts for our own journeys of faith.

Even more important, as we share in the life of the contemporary church we participate in the consequences of those responses. We look to Abraham and Sarah as the progenitors of our particular faith community. We share, especially those of us in the traditions of the American black religious experience, in the trials and tribulations of the exodus. For many in the Christian community, the celebration of the eucharist gathers us up into the never-to-be-repeated, but always recurring dying and rising of Christ. Those responses of faith in the past become the life stream for our responses in the present. They are deeply rooted in our corporate unconscious. They are located in the habits and modes of interacting with each other that we do not fully realize. They nurture our own searching. They challenge us in our unfaithfulness. They may call us into question when we have strayed. They pull us, at the same time, into what Brueggeman has called the process of "living toward a vision."[16]

In the activities of our own responding to people's responses to God's initiative in the past and present, the roles, methods, and structures that have become the educational trappings of our churches are put in proper perspective. For, in responding to God's initiative, the offensive character of the love, the justice, the compassion, and the truth of God shatter any pretensions we may have regarding the supremacy or ultimacy of the theological doctrines or educational theories we hold dear, the faithfulness of our responses, the clarity and certainty of our objectives, or the efficacy of our methods or institutions. Instead, the primary reference point for our teaching and learning is to be found in the responses of the community of faith to the initiative of God—ever calling us into new and uncharted territories and relationships—even as we are ourselves engaged in the mutual tasks of teaching and learning.

The Nature of Community

During the late eighteenth century and throughout the nineteenth century, two theories about the relation of the individual to his or her cultural milieu significantly influenced Western and white thought. The first, Romanticism, primarily associated with Jean Jacques Rousseau, viewed culture as the evil factor in a person's life. If a person could only be nurtured in an environment untainted by the corrupt influences of culture, such a person would be able to step into the course of adult affairs untainted by the baser characteristics of humanity. The second theory may be traced to John Locke, who viewed the newborn child as entering the world with a mind like a *tabula rasa,* or blank slate, upon which we might impress those values, commitments and concepts we deemed most significant.

These two views often became highly interrelated in subsequent thought. Their creative potential is evident in the development of many new insights into human nature during the past century and a half. At the same time, Rousseau's view perpetuated a naïveté about the corporate dimension of the experience of being human. The second view promulgated an unwarranted optimism about the potential effectiveness of the interventions of teachers, parents, pastors, and later, social workers, psychologists, and psychiatrists, and their capacity to mold and influence the lives of those with whom they worked. As Clyde Kluckholn has reminded us, "Perhaps the most important implication of culture . . . is the profound truth that you can never start with a clean slate so far as human beings are concerned. Every person is born into a world defined by already existing culture patterns."[17] It is inconceivable to understand any social entity without reference to its past. Even in the midst of vast social disruption, characteristic human responses will persist.

So, as I begin to explicate the meaning of the nature of community, it is to its corporate character that I first direct our attention. My approach is not a sociological one, although certain insights from the social sciences will be useful and pertinent. I am more interested in discovering what lies beneath the surface of the usual inquiries we make into what Evans has aptly described as our fascination with "turf" and "task." It is my own contention that such explorations are useful in identifying existing patterns of human relationships, but they are relatively unhelpful in locating either the authentic sources of our expectations for being in community, or the power of the intimacy we occasionally experience in our relationships with others.

Perhaps we have followed for too long and too intently the provocative contrast between society and community proposed by Ferdinand Toennies, a German sociologist writing during the 1880s. In his attempt to clarify the structure of human interaction, he defined *society as "a type of social relation that was primarily impersonal and characterized by deliberate choice, voluntary association, segmental encounters, defined obligations, and transactions shaped by rules, promises and sanctions . . . ." His view of "community" included the personal aspects of human relationships caught up in "bonds of kinship, locality, and common tasks in which human transactions are informed by consensus and tradition."*[18] Toennies' distinction has certainly helped us to understand the more obvious and structured aspects of our common life. But it has blinded us to the unofficial contribution to our corporate experience made by children and others whose roles and status are considered marginal. One consequence, according to Evans, has been the tendency to ignore the "nonstructured" modes of human relationships that often enliven and renew our social life.[19]

Similarly, this distinction strips the image of community of much of its potential. By dividing the turf of society from the task of community, the latter is all too often disengaged from the wealth of traditions and meanings that lie beneath the surface of our conscious awareness. We consequently find ourselves continuing the quest for that interrelatedness, that "commune-ality," that intensity reflected in the "community" portrayed in such records as The Acts of the Apostles. We find ourselves longing for an experience of community caught in the corporate "we," rather than the depersonalized "it." When it does not occur, we often discount the images we encounter in the New Testament as an impossible dream and look upon the institutional church as a haven for hypocrisy.

Community is, in fact, a multidimensional phenomenon. First of all, from a theological perspective, it emerges from within and through the accumulated experience of people from the past who have responded to the initiative of God. The hymnist captures this historical perspective in the familiar words, "faith of our fathers [and mothers] living still." The creeds call it "the communion of saints." It is caught up in the convenantal promise between God and Abraham and Sarah and all their descendants (Gen. 17)—a relationship formed in the past, yet ever new with each succeeding generation. Such a perspective telescopes the relationship of past and present, thereby blurring the distinctions between them. It pulls the past into the present by introducing old meanings and expectations into new events and circumstances. At the same time, it thrusts the present into the past, preparing the ground for the reinterpretation of ancient insights and experiences.

Community, moreover, is present in the relationships that exist among all people, but as a community of faith for Christians, it is especially caught up in their common allegiance to Christ as the head of the church, in the awareness that, where two or three are gathered, the binding presence of God in Christ is also present. One might call this the horizontal, or relational, dimension of community. It may be most evident in the structures and programs we create to order and perpetuate the bonds of our corporate interests and concerns.

Community is also found in the interstices of life. It takes place in those liminal experiences when our reliance upon structures, laws, and the mores of our particular cultural context are suspended, and we are gathered up into an encounter with what the church has historically called the Holy

Spirit. It is to the explication of these three dimensions of community that we now turn.

Historical Sources of Community

In order to explore the historical sources of community, let us return to the place Abraham and Sarah occupy in the faith, as well as political history, of the ancient Hebrews and contemporary Jews. From ancient times into the present, they have been identified as the father and mother of a people or nation. Even when scattered throughout the world, their descendants have not lost the unity of their common heritage. As Christians, we claim (with Paul) that Abraham and Sarah are also the progenitors of our own relationship with God and all creation by means of our baptism into the body of Christ.

Our ties to the progenitors of our faith community are not a literal geneological line of descent like that given for Jesus in the New Testament, showing his place and inheritance in the Hebrew community. Indeed, we are nurtured in a direct and experiential manner that transcends the structures of local churches and of Sunday schools or parochial schools. Those who share in the solidarity of the community of faith have a sense of intimate dependence upon the faith of the saints. Perhaps, as mentioned earlier, this dynamic is nowhere more dramatically illustrated than in the earthy and comforting words of the spiritual, "Rock-a My Soul in the Bosom of Abraham." In singing this song, we acknowledge that we are a people gathered into, and under, the identity of a man whose responses to God, along with those of Sarah, have helped shape the faith of people through the ages. Take note of the physical aspects of the imagery in this song. They draw us back into the most significant of all formative interactions between parent and child—those physical patterns of touching and holding that lay the groundwork for the trust Erik Erikson has called the basic developmental task in the process of becoming function-ing people. Rocking in the bosom of another gathers up the image and the experience of the power that is transferred from one person to another when one is surrounded, protected, sustained, and loved.

That spiritual, in other words, projects a common experience in our lives that actually transcends the immediacy of our own experience. Because it is not tied to the events of our own lives, but reveals how our lives are engaged in the corporate phenomenon of being human, the song blurs the distinctions we so often make between things of the present and things of the past or future. That experience, caught up in the words of a haunting song, elicits responsive chords from people of all ages and in all circumstances. Carl Jung calls the experience of this sort of archetypal human relationship "participation." In Jungian theory, participation is much more than mere involvement in an activity. Rather it is "an unconscious process expressing the way in which the unconscious thinks."[20] It is a process that arises from the springs of the collective well of human history, affecting all of our idiosyncratic thoughts and actions. It blurs the distinctions of time and underscores the tenacity and persistence of ties binding us into a fellowship that cannot be fragmented by structures of race, culture, and nationality, or economic and social distinctions.

A brief digression may be in order to clarify Jung's view of the unconscious in order to understand more clearly his use of the word *participation*. He postulated that the psyche has three layers. The layer that is known to each of us is consciousness— the fragile strata of attitudes with which we approach our "immediate external environment." It contains the "basic orientation" for our lives and for our roles in society. It provides the starting point for any rational or logical analysis we may employ in ordering either our thought or experience.[21]

Beneath the layer of consciousness lies the personal unconscious. It contains those elements that have been repressed and forgotten, as well as those drives and desires that have not yet reached consciousness. Some of the content of the personal unconscious is often brought to our attention in a family reunion when the older members of the family start telling stories on the rest of us—stories that have been lost to memory, or confused with recollections of other events. This second layer is obviously highly personal. Because it includes only our own experiences and our perceptions of them, it is unique for each of us.

The largest component of the psyche is also the one most deeply embedded in the human experience. Jung called it the collective unconscious. W. Lloyd Warner, an anthropologist, has described it as the "'eternal' nature of the human species."[22] As one of Jung's students has emphasized, the collective unconscious functions much like a deep reservoir. It is the "source of the materials that come into consciousness and as the point of contact between the individual and the greater-than-individual forces in life. The fundamental hypothesis on which Jung works is the idea that the potentialities within the individual personality are not left unaffected by the developments of history, and that what happens in time leaves its mark not only on the psyche of the individual, but also on the continuity of the human race."[23]

Consequently, when we speak of participation in the collectivity of human history as one of the sources of the community of faith, we do so with our sensitivities heightened by Jung's perceptions. As images from the reservoir of the experience of the human race well up into our individual psyches, traditional distinctions between past and present are often blurred. New events are filled with meanings deeply rooted in our corporate past. Images from the past shape our perceptions of, and consequently our responses to, the events in our present.

In other words, images shaping our thoughts, feelings, and actions emerge from the depths of the historical human experience, breaking through our patterns of speaking, our unquestioned but deeply rooted values and beliefs, and our behavior, to reveal our commonality with others around the world, with those who preceded us, and with those who will live long after we have been forgotten. These images do not appear in any orderly and logical manner. Instead, they often intrude into the structures of our daily lives, much as the call of God to

Samuel interrupted his sleep, or the vision of Isaiah intruded upon the routines of his priestly activities, or the discovery of the sacred book jogged the dusty memories of Josiah and his contemporaries.

We may encounter these corporate or common images in the not-so-private chamber of our dreams. We discover them in the rituals and symbols of peoples everywhere. We see them in the play of children. Jung was impressed by the repetition of these images across age, cultural, and religious lines. They point to the common bond of being human. Even more, they reveal the corporate framework for our personal identities.

A conversation between two central characters in John Steinbeck's *The Winter of Our Discontent* may illustrate my point. In trying to explain why the Twenty-third Psalm could still make his stomach turn over, put a flutter in his chest and light a fire in his brain, one man describes his relation to the formative power of the church. "Let's say that when I was a little baby, and all my bones soft and malleable, I was put in a small Episcopal cruciform box and so took my shape. Then, when I broke out of the box, the way a baby chick escapes an egg, is it strange that I had the shape of a cross?"[24]

The stories of our emerging identities are as common as his. We may assert our individuality, but we repeatedly reveal the links between ourselves and the depths of the human experience. Sydney Mead, building on Erik Erikson's discussion of identity, underscores this historical premise for personal identity. He observes that our identities are grounded in a "sense of solidarity with an historical people, a community that transcends the individual in both time and space."[25] We are for the most part unconscious of this corporate framework that links us to the past, locates us in the present, and serves as a springboard into the future. Yet this social milieu surrounds and nurtures us like the air we breathe. Even when unaware of its presence, we do not exist as human beings without it. Participation in the flow of human experience, in other words, is the ground for being human. Hence, one source for the community of faith may be found in the history of the race and in its continual quest for a relationship with the mystery that exists beyond our understanding, yet permeates our daily lives, giving them meaning and direction.

Relational Sources of Community

The corporate character of our response to God's actions of love and justice may not only be traced to the commonality of images and symbols deeply embedded in the unconscious depths of humanity. It may also be located in our relationships encompassing our interactions in space and across time, and structured into institutions, societies, and family networks.

Relationships are basic to the human experience. Indeed, from a Christian perspective at least, a person exists only in relationship with others. This theme is not only central to the creation story in the interactions between human beings and their Creator, but it is to be found in the necessary interdependence of man and woman, both for their personal well-being and for the future of the race.

Social and biological scientists have reinforced this historic tenet of Judeo-Christian belief when reporting research findings to the effect that the intellectual and emotional growth of infants is diminished significantly, if not irreversibly, when children do not have adequate interactions with other people. Similarly, our spiritual growth is shaped significantly by the quality of the nurturing relationships in the earliest years of our lives.

If we accept Erik Erikson's thesis that trust is the basic learning task upon which all other developmental learning tasks are built, the necessity of trusting relationships in early childhood is crucial for all later spiritual growth. Trust establishes the framework through which we may risk the unknown demands of each new day and situation. It provides the springboard for the leaps we make into the mysteries of life. It frees us to acknowledge our dependence upon forces and powers we cannot ultimately know. It undergirds us when we are called out of the perceived safety and security of our immediate environment into that which is new and still to be explored.

The phenomenon of "being called" into relationships with others is dramatically but simply revealed in the actions of most children as they begin to take their first steps. Parents, siblings, others proffer a hand to demonstrate that security and stability do exist beyond that chasm of several inches separating the two people. With an encouraging word, the child is "called out" to take a step. In similar reciprocal acts of being called out and calling out to others, we acknowledge and affirm the significance of each other's presence. There is a sense of interdependence in our togetherness. This experience is described as "fellowship" by some Christians, a relationship that involves mutuality, or a sense of being together in a common action.

Hence, an experience in the community of faith involves more than the presence of two or more people. Rather it engages two or more distinctive individuals—an "I" and a "Thou," as Martin Buber has said. Such a relationship does not involve the fusion of personalities. Instead, in the interaction of being "called out," we participate in a two-way process. Someone calls. Another responds. The interaction is repeated, with the roles changing back and forth in a process of reciprocity.

In such an encounter we experience the intimate bonding of ourselves to each other. It conveys to us the impression that we are participating in something transcending the finitude of our own boundaries. And yet, in that very closeness, we also discern our inability to share our friend or neighbor's experience. All we are able to receive is a description of it.

Interdependence conveys the "push and pull" of both closeness and distance, or intimacy and separation. In our mutuality, we are still distinct, sometimes even alone although we are with one another. This interdependence is not limited to any phase of our lives. It is as common to us in our childhood as it is in our adulthood. And it is also found in the relationships of children and adults. How often we experience in the same moment the hug of a child pulling the two of us into an intense and mystical embrace and the child's resistance, clearly announcing that she or he is not to be subsumed in our strength, overwhelmed by our size, or consumed by our love.

The relational sources for community are undoubtedly most thoroughly described by anthropologists in their discussions of enculturation. These are the subtle influences transmitting behavior patterns, attitudes, values, beliefs, and perceptions across the generations, who usually have little consciousness of either their presence or the processes involved. A simple illustration may convey the potential and power of these processes of transmission. A friend, upon observing my father, my son, and me walking across a field one day, later described the uncanny similarities in our gait and stride. Differences in age, in the regions of the country we each grew up in, and the years separating our visits with each other did not seem to have much influence on the transmission of this pattern in our behavior. Granted the importance of our common genetic heritage, of even greater significance were the imitative processes—based upon the centrality of one person to another—conveying the message "how one walked."

Similarly, the rites, rituals, values, and perceptions of the nature of the sacred are handed down from one generation to the next and from one people to the next, often with little attention to the means of transmission. These patterns may be seen in the simplest and most common of the habits of our spiritual disciplines. The postures of prayer, for example, are rarely "taught" by formal instruction. They are entered into as children join parents and other adults in the acts of praying. They are appropriated through imitation and repetition. They are conveyed from one generation to the next through the authority of the relationship between young and old.

Many of the relationships that give meaning and structure to a community, however, extend beyond the circle of people who are known and can be seen, touched, or heard. A black student helped me to "get inside" this phenomenon initially in a discussion regarding certain "brothers and sisters" who lived more than a hundred years ago. These people, as real to him as his siblings and the members of his own local church, whom he also called brothers and sisters, were not ancestors. Instead, all they shared happened to be the common heritage of slavery and descent from the continent of Africa. Despite his location in time, his relative affluence and formal education, he belonged to that experience of yesterday as well. He carried many of their scars on his back and their hope in his heart in his perception of contemporary events, in the use of his knowledge to explore issues, and in his interactions with other people. His relationship to those "brothers and sisters" transformed his perception of his life as well as of life in general. With the eyes of the black American experience he looked upon the world around him responding from the depths of that experience to all he encountered. His decisions and actions could not be limited to the data of twentieth-century American life. Instead, they revealed as well his interactions with the experience of people over the past two hundred years.

The relationship of the "I" and the "Thou" is not necessarily limited to those we can see, hear, and touch. Perhaps now we can begin to comprehend the mystical and powerful personal relationship some people have to the great figures of the faith in the past. Although it is often treated in sentimental fashion, there is a profound recognition of this facet of our faith-lives in the familiar words of the hymn, "What a Friend We Have in Jesus." This Jesus is the same Jesus who knew and was known by the disciples, a host of others down through the ages, and by many today. It is the same Jesus who wandered along the shores of Galilee and through Capernaum calling people out to follow him. It is the same Jesus whose presence has the power to rivet our attention and to direct our actions. It is the same Jesus whose meaning to us has been transformed by the cross and through the encounters of those first followers with the risen Lord. In our own relationship with that historic, yet symbolic figure, we find ourselves sharing distinctive but common experiences. In responding to his call, "Follow me," we participate in a distinctive community of relationships that transform those we experience in our families, neighborhoods, and congregations.

The relational dimension of human experience, however, is usually made explicit in structures. Our bonds are confirmed by the ties of family, neighborhood, and social class. They are reinforced by creeds, constitutions, and codes of conduct. They are organized into institutions, organizations, and fellowships. These structures give order to our relationships. They clarify lines of authority and status and give credibility to what we do through the roles we fill in and through our relationships.

These structures enhance as well as inhibit our relationships. They influence our conduct and attitudes. They locate us in time and space. In other words, they make our interactions concrete and tangible. In so doing, our lives are undergirded by certain securities. We can rely upon these structures, up to a point at least, to give order and continuity to our days. We do not need to create from scratch each event and each relationship in each new encounter.

These bonds are crucial. Without them, a community cannot exist. Perhaps it is at this point that we can see the significance of the institutional church's linking past and future and embodying our hopes for significant relationships in the present. Congregations gather people together, nurture them into relationships received from the past, and prepare them to assume responsibility for those who have not yet entered into their fellowship. Smaller groups intensify those relationships in and for the moment, and denominational agencies structure our interconnectedness with people throughout the world and across the centuries. Because these structures are the most obvious component in community to us, however, they often take on an importance they do not merit. They are only means to the continuity of the race, not the goal toward which we strive. And yet, neither can their significance be underestimated, as is often the case when congregations decide to discard their traditions. These bonds, in all their finitude, provide humanity with the resources to create in microcosm the order and harmony intended by God for all of creation.

Spontaneous Sources of Community

A third source for the corporate nature of the community of faith may be found in people's spontaneous and immediate responses to the initiative of God that breaks in upon the obvious structures of our common life, filling them with hope, new meaning, and power. This third source of community was ignored by Toennies in his distinction between "society" and "community." Yet, it is expressed in such images as Auden's "for the time being," or the biblical "in the fullness of time," or in the popular idiom, "time seemed to stand still." As Richard Tholin has pointed out, in the Old Testament these outbreakings of community were often associated with the power of God working through the words and deeds of prophets. As a response to the will of God, the prophetic word became the event through which the people encountered "God's ultimate purposes and immediate demands," which shaped, in turn, "the flow of history—as the fear of prophetic proclamation by political leaders made abundantly clear."[26]

The prophetic encounter as event broke through the structures of society with little regard for their propriety. It ignored the rituals governing the relationships of people and classes of people. It confronted individuals with little regard for status or station in life. It introduced a vision of life transcending the mundane objectives of the structures and organizations of life. It conveyed a sense of power and authority that had to be taken seriously.

Victor W. Turner in *The Ritual Process* describes such events as consisting of a blend of "lowliness and sacredness, of homogeneity and comradeship." Particularly in certain rites, "we are presented . . . with a 'moment in and out of time,'" which is at the same time "in and out of secular social structure."[27] In this moment "we experience time" as depth, "as having quality as well as quantity . . . ." We do not note "its duration," Fred Buechner has observed. We concentrate upon "its content."[28] Turner calls this experience *"communitas,"* to differentiate it from our more common use of *community* to describe a sociological and geographical entity.

39

In his discussion of "The Quest for Community," Robert A. Evans has noted that "communitas . . . can never be created—only celebrated." It is not "a possession; it is a gift. It is not a state, but a moment." Moreover it is "not segmented; it is wholistic *[sic]*. It is not hierarchical, but rather egalitarian," because each participant in the event submits to the authority of the transcendent intrusion upon our finite experience.[29] For a moment, we encounter together the stillness of time and the intimacy of infinity. And in the process we lose contact with distinctions of age, race, class, or nation. We become, in the words of the popular song, "one in the Spirit."

It is undoubtedly this often powerful and dramatic experience of being *with* others that people long for in their search for fellowship or community and in their continuing efforts to "will" it into existence. In seeking to experience communitas, we in the church, as well as many in the larger culture we are a part of, engage in exhaustive measures to create it. We establish atmospheres and choose procedures to emphasize the presence of mystery. We have learned how to create artificial experiences of community with the techniques employed in revivals, sensitivity training, and with the aid of technology of light and sound, or the use of drugs to alter our states of consciousness. But such efforts always lead to an artificial and contrived event, perhaps most dramatically illustrated in Orwell's *1984*. They lack the power to be found in events of communitas.

Communitas, to the contrary, "emerges here and there" and only "from time to time."[30] Any attempt to structure, organize, or guarantee its presence will be its undoing or will contribute to our manipulation of others.[31] All the organizing that we in the church do to effect some experience of communitas—whether it be in small groups, through a revival meeting, around some mission or evangelical task, some fellowship activity, or some study of our heritage—cannot and will not create community in this sense. Such efforts are important, however, because they may prepare for, or be a consequence of, that event of communitas. They may call us to be open to the unexpected and to celebrate the gift of past experiences of communitas. These humanly contrived events, however, prove to be a poor substitute for the unexpected surprises of the Spirit that intrude into our common life from time to time.

Events of communitas are possible partly because the structures embodied in our laws, customs, rituals, creeds, social stratifications, and institutional organizations are not as rigid as they often appear to be. There are recurring transitional moments, events Turner describes as *liminal*,[32] when people move from one era to the next, or from one status to another. The relentless changes in our lives due to the passage of time offer these liminal occasions for our reflection and celebration. Perhaps the most common such event takes place each year on our birthday. The party, the familiar rituals of song, cake, cards, and gifts, all serve to focus our attention upon the life of a given person. Often the event opens up new possibilities. After age five, one begins school. The sixteenth birthday often means one can now drive a car. The eighteenth signifies one has reached voting age. Slogans abound around certain years. A person is "over the hill" at thirty, although life "begins at forty," and so on. But common to each celebrated birthday is the potential to be filled with new energy, or "life anew" as the hymn claims.

Communitas occurs in the midst of the structures of our lives by infusions of vitality (as Turner has emphasized) from the *margins* of those structures.[33] The most evident illustration of this phenomenon may be seen in the various civil rights movements of the past twenty-five years. The sense of unity and fellowship, the overwhelming power of the cause, the sense of shaping destiny mark the songs, chants, speeches, and reflections of the participants. "We shall overcome" became not only a theme song for many, it also represented the intrusion of those living on the margins of our society into its mainstream. In a manner not unlike the sounds of the trumpets of Joshua's band marching around the walls of Jericho, that song and its singers penetrated many of the walls separating race from race, class from class. To those attempting to preserve the traditional structures, the situation—marches, chants, songs—had all the appearances of war. The experience had a dramatically different appearance to those on the margins who were participating in the marches. It often seemed to be a grand happening—a celebration. Caught up in the message "we shall overcome," they experienced an intense and clear sense of purpose, cohesiveness, and power. Such events have repeatedly altered the course of history. Their spontaneity has gathered up many who felt most loyal to the structures of the past and released them to respond in fresh ways to the demands of the new age in which they found themselves.

The release of the power of the marginal is a dominant biblical theme. It is found in the servant motif, in the claim that the captives shall be released, in the renewing power of those journeys from the outside to claim and reclaim the promised land. It is the hope continually offered to the blind, the sick, and the imprisoned of the world in any time and in any place.

Turner speaks of yet a third source of communitas. It is found in *inferiority*—in those who have little or no status.[34] Children are among the most obvious people in this category. They have yet to jump through the hoops every society creates to mark their arrival at an acceptable level of maturity. And yet, in their "inferior" status, children also intrude upon the patterns and structures of our daily lives. The birth of a child can reduce men who never cry to tears. The spontaneous hug of a child can disarm a proper and dignified adult. Not long ago I saw the power in a young child who not only led his elders, but transformed the content of the structure of a Sunday morning service of worship.

This incident happened on a Christmas day that fell on a Sunday. The manger and straw from the previous evening's pageant had been left in front of the altar. A large doll representing the infant Jesus lay "sleeping" in the manger. Just as the pastor began his sermon, a two-year-old child who had been present the previous evening broke away from his parents to "see the baby Jesus." For more than ten minutes this young disciple—without a sound—gazed upon the baby, finally touching the baby's face gently. He then sat upon the floor in front of the manger as if waiting with the infant Jesus. He finally returned to his parents. We of course do not know what was going on in the mind of the child. But in sharing the experience with each other later, members of that congregation were caught up in a visit to the manger that happened nearly two thousand years ago and yet occurred only a few minutes before. Through the experiences of one child, a congregation was led to a fresh encounter with the Christ event.

In events of communitas, the inferior are often the leaders. The leader may be a child, as Isaiah indicated. The leader may be a pilgrim or clown, two childlike roles often assumed by adults. Those who take on these roles consciously choose to relate to the structures of existence as "inferior"—people without power and status. They have chosen to relate to life with the openness, wonder, and naïveté we often associate with childlikeness. They may become the agents of those spontaneous moments of community erupting in our midst, because they perceive the hidden but ever-present mysteries and surprises lurking around every corner. They are not embarrassed or reticent about acknowledging that they see that the emperor is wearing no clothes, or that the flight of a butterfly brightens an otherwise gray day, or that a lonely person needs a hug. They introduce spontaneity into the routine, laughter into the dreary, beauty into the drab. As Turner has emphasized, "communitas is of the now." It captures the elements of spontaneity and immediacy in human experience. As such, it contrasts with the structures of our society, which are rooted in the relationships and processes of the past and extend into the future through "language, law, and custom."[35] Communitas, in other words, breaks "through the interstices of structure, in liminality; at the edges of structure, in marginality; and from beneath structure, in inferiority. It is almost everywhere held to be sacred or 'holy,' possibly because it transgresses or dissolves the norms that govern structured and institutionalized relationships and is accompanied by experiences of unprecedented potency."[36]

The experience of communitas is obviously not a private one. It involves the gathering up of our corporate and common life. It is, in the best sense, "a happening"—an event in the now in which all eternity is present. As such it is an eschatological event, embodying a movement from the beyond into the here and now, from the infinite into the finite, moving the "coming age into the present," and linking "contemporary events firmly to their consummation."[37] Such a perspective establishes a vision for life that penetrates the structures guiding and influencing our lives.

That vision is no "pie in the sky" that will come in some "sweet by and by." It is a vision revealed in "the present moment as the fullness of time." It "transforms the ordinary day into the dawn of the Lord's day."[38] Such an event confronts us with the limits of our own experience. It presents us with the need for confession and repentance, for the turnaround that Christians have historically called conversion. It is a time for choosing and for celebrating the presence of God.

Such an event may well be a public event. Pentecost would certainly fit that description. It may be a personal experience similar to that in the life of Saul/Paul while traveling on the road to Damascus, or in the religious pilgrimage of John Wesley who left Aldersgate Chapel with his "heart strangely warmed" after encountering the Living Word. But it is always a corporate event. It pulls people back into community. It does not remove them from fellowship with others. It reminds them of their shared humanness.

Communitas, in other words, is shared. Even in our most private moments of prayer and meditation, in communitas we are surrounded by a cloud of witnesses. It is a remembered event transmitted by story, ritual, and creed to subsequent generations. It is a social and cultural event transforming lives and relationships and often ecclesiastical structures and political processes. Simply reflecting on the lives of the apostles after the Resurrection and after Pentecost, or on the life of Paul, illustrates this dynamic. Communitas, in other words, exists in the interstices of our daily lives, transforming our structures, routines, and rituals. It is the creative spirit of God present.

Summary

As we reflect on the nature and meaning of the experience of community in and through which we may begin to explore the nature and function of the church's teaching ministry, we cannot limit our understanding to any one of these sources (historical, relational, spontaneous) of that experience. For the community that gathers up people's responses to the initiative of God may be traced to the unknown depths of those responses in ages past that continue to fill our imaginations and to shape our perceptions. It may be found in our relationships not only in the immediacy of a given church fellowship, but also in the sequence of structured relationships that crosses the ages from the days of Abraham and Sarah into the present. It conveys the living bonds of fellowship closely binding all of us into one great fellowship of love and justice. And it may be made manifest in those moments of corporate responsiveness interrupting the structures and processes of our daily lives—creating a vision of what is possible, yet demonstrating its fulfillment in the present. It is in the continuous interaction of these sources that children and other childlike people may be taught the truth and grace of God's continuing creative and redemptive activity in the history of humankind.

CHAPTER 2

ON BEING
CHILDREN
A Biblical Perspective

What does it mean to be children of God? Certainly not to live as children often did in the communities of ancient Israel or the early church. Indeed, from the vantage point of twentieth-century humanitarian standards, most children in the Bible lived under inhumane and oppressive conditions. Disease and early death constantly hovered over their lives. Adults often treated them in a fashion we would describe as legally abusive. Sons were valued more highly than daughters, and the first-born son was treated with greater respect than subsequent sons. When this pattern was broken, as in Joseph's family, violence was often the result. Children were sold into slavery. They were sacrificed. They were the spoils of war and the victims of political intrigue. The lot of children in the Bible, in other words, is not a particularly pleasant or pretty picture.

In spite of the abusive and oppressive treatment of children often recorded in the biblical narrative, the Israelites developed at the same time an understanding of the meaning of childhood that continues to have power for us today. It provides the framework for our contemporary approaches to safeguarding the welfare of children. It undergirds the commitment of men and women to take the nurture of children seriously. It inspires efforts to reform the social conditions and institutions impoverishing children's lives. It feeds the compassion of those attempting to respond to the special needs of children. It is not my intent here, however, to explore biblical perspectives on childhood for programmatic suggestions and guidelines for our work with children in the church. My purpose is to explore the symbolic function of children in Israelite thought and life. This approach, I contend, may not only help us discern something of the special place and function children held in that ancient society, it may also help us to clarify what it means for people of all ages to be children of God in this day and in this place. That perspective may not only amplify our understanding of the nature of community, it may help us explore the community of faith's responsibility to teach people of all ages to participate in contemporary life as empowered members of the community of faith and as reconciling agents of God's redemptive work.

When viewed symbolically, the special functions of children transcend both the particularities of their behavior and the specific treatment they receive from family, neighbors, and the culture in which they live. This perspective is especially true of the biblical view of children. The Bible tends to view all people as children, no matter what their age or station in life. Anyone who was a member of the nation was considered to be a child of Israel. Kings were called sons of God. Jesus was also called "son of God." Paul refers to new Christians as children. To be a child in this sense did not limit one's behavior to that of a given stage in a person's life. Rather, it signifies the "constant dependence" of human beings upon God. In fact, G. Ernest Wright has observed that, from a biblical perspective, the meaning and destiny of human life are "determined entirely by this dependence and by what God is and does."[1] Reinhold Neibuhr, in his classic study of human nature, makes the same point. In both Old and New Testaments, he observed the "brevity and dependence of all temporal existence" is contrasted to the "majesty and eternity of God."[2]

To be called a child of God, in other words, clarified the nature of the divine-human relationship. From this perspective two important but quite different images of children from the New Testament begin to make sense. On the one hand we encounter Paul's advice that we are to give up childish things in our maturing faith (I Cor. 13:11). On the other hand, we are confronted by the admonition of Jesus. Unless we become like small children, we will not receive the kingdom of heaven (Matt. 19:14, Mark 10:14, Luke 18:16). The quest for understanding the meaning of being a child of God and of approaching faith in a childlike (but not childish) manner, therefore, becomes the focus of our next two chapters. This chapter will explore what it means to be a child of God.

Children Are Gifts from God

In the first place, the Israelites viewed the child as a gift from God. On this point, the biblical record is quite explicit. The Psalmist proclaims, "Children are a gift from the Lord" (Ps. 127:3, GNB). The birth, especially of the first-born, was cause for celebration. Joy filled the household of Abraham and Sarah upon the birth of Isaac, the household of Jacob and Rachel upon the birth of Joseph, and the household of Elkanah and Hannah upon the birth of Samuel. For the gospel writer, the unbridled excitement over the birth of Jesus could only be captured in the alleluias of the heavenly host.

Conversely, sterility was considered to be a trial, a time of chastisement, or at least a sign of disgrace in the community and before God.[3] This view obviously emerged in the primitive environment of ancient Israel when children were crucial for the continuity of the family name and fortune, in the establishment of a society that needed soldiers as well as men and women to solidify a claim upon the occupied land and to provide the labor needed to maintain the family enterprise.

In our own day, when our minds are preoccupied with the problems of overpopulation, the starvation of vast segments of humanity, and the scarcity of basic needs for survival, sterility—either natural or chosen—may not necessarily be a sign of unfaithfulness. But to view children—no matter whose children they may be—as less than the gift of God may still be seen as a sign of unfaithfulness. For the child is not a gift only to the parents. The child is first and foremost a gift to the community. The baptismal vows of many churches reaffirm this principle. The child is born into the nurture and care of humanity. A particular family is *entrusted* with the care of the child. A congregation surrounds the family with its support and care. It covenants with God to serve as an environment of love, compassion, justice, and hope for that child as a representative of all children. Unfortunately, this view (found in the words of most baptismal celebrations) rarely penetrates the consciousness of clergy, parents, or congregation. Hence all too many people do not look upon the baptized child as a gift and sign of God's creative and redemptive love to the community and fail to abide by the congregational vow to be responsible for the child. It should be no surprise, then, that as we age we also do not tend to view the men and women who surround us as gifts of God to the community to be celebrated, treated with respect, and surrounded with nurturing love.

The biblical record does not look upon the child as an object to possess, to love, or to raise up according to our own whims. The Israelite view of the meaning of personhood challenges this all too typical approach to raising our own children. For in the birth of a child we do not simply observe the creative consequence of a sexual union of a man and a woman. We encounter the re-presentation of the creative spirit of God. Indeed from a biblical perspective, a child exists only as a direct consequence of God's life-giving action initiated in the course of creation.

In the Genesis creation story, the narrator describes how God molded a creature from the clay of the earth and breathed life into it. That perspective dominates all subsequent perceptions of the source of our personhood. The Israelite had little interest in identifying the various elements in a person. Unlike the Greeks, who often made distinctions within the person among body, mind and spirit, the Israelites tended to make distinctions between people based upon their place within the community. They did not understand any part of the experience of a given child without perceiving that child in his or her context. As J. Pederson has argued, the Hebrews did not really believe they knew someone until a person could be seen against the whole of his or her background. That information provides a way of seeing the meaning and relationship of the way a person speaks, moves, and acts. A person is known not just as Saul, for example. He is only known in his totality when he is perceived as "Saul, the son of Kish . . . because 'Kish, the rich peasant,' is also known for his importance" in the tribe of Benjamin and for the place he occupies in the history of his family.[4] Ultimately, such a person is known most fully as a son of Abraham, or as a child of God. From this perspective, the narrator of the creation story reminds each of us who read or hear the story that the people of God are more than the fragile physical structures we can see, touch, hear, and smell. Rather they, and we, live and move and are known to each other because we live in a context of historical, political, social, and economic relationships. Even more, we all trace the vitality of our living to the creative breath of God.

With this view as a part of our heritage (albeit one often lost to us), we should not be surprised when we look upon the birth of a child with wonder and awe. We still do not consider it strange in our scientific world to marvel at the mystery of new life. It should not be unexpected that, in spite of the pain of childbirth, many people experience the birth of a child as a hallowed event—a re-presentation of "emmanuel" or God-with-us. Indeed, one might view the birth narratives of Jesus as paradigmatic for the birth of all children.

To begin, the birth narratives underscore the special relationship that exists between all people and their Creator. Jesus is described as the Son of God. But the gospel writers and Paul emphasize that all who live in faithful relationship to the source of their creatureliness are also to be called children of God. It is a time for rejoicing. The child is surrounded by gifts. It is a time for contemplation and reflection. Mary is not the only mother to have pondered the deeper meanings of the new life in her arms. Today as in any age, it is an awesome and somewhat frightening task to introduce a child into the world. As I write these words, the newspapers are filled with news about the violence on our highways and in many homes in our land. Hostages, terrorism, assassinations, and political upheavals alter international relationships and heighten the fears of national leaders. The energy crisis continues to mount—with escalating prices, industrial intrigue, governmental timidity and consumer anxiety. There are wars in many lands. People are dying by the millions in certain sections of the globe. The nuclear armaments race continues to escalate. Herod and his troops are no greater harbingers of death and destruction than hunger, war, disease, or the institutional maltreatment of many children today. The result is the same—dying children, physically and emotionally maimed children, spiritually neglected children. Such a world must frighten any parent. It is not a world of peace into which we introduce a new child. It is a world filled with violence. We can see the violence in our hospitals, in our schools, on the streets, and on the television any day we open our eyes to the pain experienced by children. So birth is a time of reflection and contemplation for any concerned mother and father.

And yet, the birth of a child is a joyous event. Through the gift of new life we anticipate the promise of a world governed by peace and harmony. We envision a world filled with justice. We allow ourselves to be filled with hope. We listen to the music of the spheres, and we, with our loved ones, affirm the child entrusted to us. Just as the child is not ours, but God's, we acknowledge that gift in formally baptizing the child into the community that centers its life upon God. Historically at least, it is at this point that the child received a name that located him or her not only within the specific set of relationships of the family, but in the whole of space and time.

A name has a special function. It is in the recognition of their own names that children first demonstrate the capacity to be aware of God's presence. From a biblical perspective, "one makes a name alive by mentioning it."[5] That is what happens when the pastor asks for the name of the child in the service of baptism. In repeating the ancient formula, "I baptize you, Mary Jane . . .," the pastor grants that child's name legitimacy in the community. It is made to stand for the person. It represents a living vitality. This liturgical truth is grounded in a biblical view of the power of one's name. It is also seen in the importance of the name to children in their daily interactions with others.

Children look upon their names as among their most treasured possessions. They cling to them, refusing to be swayed by the games of bigger people who try to entice them to respond to other names. It locates them in a very specific place. It means the spot they occupy in the room has truly been taken by them and no one else is able to intrude upon that space.

The name places the child, moreover, into a given set of relationships. The Hebrew child was known as the son or daughter of specific parents, a fact prompting all the begats in both Old and New Testaments, as well as our own fascination with genealogies. They and we are located in our communities through the names of the families into which we are born or adopted. The name gives us a heritage as well as a place. When people receive their names, their personhood is recognized. They are granted identity that, as Margaret and David Steward have described, is the "fruit of one family and the seed of the next."[6] A person with a name is not an isolated creature. On the contrary, the newly named person stands both with and against others in the here and now. He or she also lives at the juncture of past and future generations. This perspective underscores the importance of the name in the baptism of an infant or an adult. For it locates the "new" person in a set of relationships transcending the finite and historical boundaries of our specific genealogies. It affirms our recognition of the fact that each child is indeed a child of the community—a child of God.

It is at this point that the name becomes most important. It is the means by which we are called out. It distinguishes us from those around us. Just as parents, siblings, and friends may elicit a response from a child by calling his or her name, it is through our names that we, too, recognize that we have been called out to respond to life in a unique way. In that response the content of the gift embodied in our personhood takes shape. Numerous examples of this experience abound in both Old and New Testaments. While watching sheep, Moses heard his name apparently coming from a burning bush. Through his sleep, Samuel responded to a voice calling his name. Jesus wandered through Galilee calling out first one person and then another, by name, to follow him. Saul, later called Paul, was confronted by name on the road to Damascus. Similarly, the early church singled out by name such people as Stephen to respond to the needs of the community in given ways. Through our names we are given specificity in the household of God. Through our names the gifts we represent are acknowedged and either received or rejected by the community in which we live.

Naming does not occur only upon the birth of children. When people enter a new relationship, engage in some event that alters the way they see themselves and the way others perceive them, or undergo some personal transformation, they often receive or take on a new name. The young boy who proves his prowess with a baseball bat is dubbed "Slugger" by his teammates. A woman in our culture has traditionally taken the family name of her husband in the wedding ceremony. Recently, many couples have taken each other's names to symbolize that they enter this new relationship—this new interdependent identity—as equals. Abram became Abraham and Sarai became Sarah when they entered a covenanted relationship with God. In the past, among some native American tribes, significant events in a person's life would be recognized and celebrated, and then recalled, through a new name. This granting of a new name clarifies one's new relationship to others in the community, and acknowledges the new status one has acquired. In each case, the new name represents not only a change in status, but also the community's recognition of one's new sense of identity, purpose, or mission.

In the spiritual pilgrimage, these events have variously been described as conversions, transformations, or rebirths. In such an event a person often encounters the familiar like a newborn child or a stranger. Indeed, the church has often described such people as "born again." The old appears to be new. The commonplace seems extraordinary. The experience is not unlike that described by social scientists as "culture shock." The shift in perspective brought about by a transforming event requires new modes of thinking and behaving. It takes time to absorb and to appropriate the changes involved. These transforming events often cause us to relate to the new unknown and the mysteries of life like children. We approach them tentatively, with curiosity and an openness to the future. Just as with the newborn child, this newness of spirit introduces the potential of God's creative presence in the life of the community. That presence also comes as a gift, not simply to the person, but to the community. This newness of spirit, in other words, whether through the birth of a child or the rebirth of an older person, comes to the community as a gift of the ever-creative spirit of God.

Children Are Bearers of Culture

In a literal as well as symbolic manner, children perpetuate the destiny of the family from one generation to the next through the ages, as long as there are any descendants left.[7] Pederson reminds us that for the Israelite, the "strong cohesion of the family" across the years extends both "upwards and downwards." The family is not simply identified by its relationship to its founder. It is, from the Hebraic patriarchal perspective, a "house of fathers," a symbolic way of identifying the contribution of each generation with the "peculiar essence" of the family.[8] The significance of continuity in the family may be seen in such Hebraic laws as those that protected a man from serving in the military until he had a son to perpetuate the family name, or in the marriage of a childless widow to her husband's brother so that she might have the opportunity to bear a child who would perpetuate the family name. Children, in other words, were crucial to the Hebrew people because they gave evidence of the strength of the family and assured its continuity into the future.

Through the children of the family, the values received from the past are impressed onto the future. This view is basic to the

Israelite view that the family is the cornerstone of the Israelite community. As Pederson has noted, for the Israelite, "every community is a community of kinsmen with a common ancestor." This ancestor is the "bearer of the unity" of the community. Abraham is perhaps the most obvious, even archetypal, example. Such a leader stamps the house or community with his personality. He is called its "father, and those who join him are his sons."[9] Hence, from a biblical perspective, each family and community bears the imprint of its founder in its character. Anyone who rejected the values of the founder imbedded in the life of the family or group would expect to be disinherited. A sense of loyalty, unity, and homogeneity consequently transcends time and place.

Perhaps it is at this point that I should clarify some of the differences to be found between our relationship to God as creator of all people, and our relationship to Abraham and Sarah as symbolic ancestors of our own household or community of faith. On the one hand, all of us have been stamped with the imprint of the divine image. We are creatures of God. From the biblical perspective, God acts *like* a parent-figure, distributing both justice and mercy. In our human experience we are as children in comparison with the vastness of the resources and capabilities of our Creator to respond to any and all human needs. We may each relate to God directly as individuals and as members of the human family. But that relationship, no matter how old or mature we may be, still reflects the dynamic of a parent-child relationship. The impatience of a Paul, the resistance of a Jeremiah, the frustration of a Moses, the petulance of a Peter only illustrate the childishness in the faithfulness of the most revered saints of the past. Similarly, the unwavering trust of an Elijah contending with the prophets of Baal, the singlemindedness of a St. Francis, or the compassion of a Mother Theresa exemplify the richest strains of childlikeness. Such a relationship is a theological one. It describes something of our experience of the nature of God, and only by indirection do we discover something about who we are.

When I refer to Abraham as the father of the Israelite people or of ourselves as spiritual descendents of Abraham and Sarah, my comments are informed more by insights from anthropology than theology. For when we describe our relationship to Abraham, we are clarifying the way that we view ourselves as a people, a culture or movement. Our unity is to be found in the processes of enculturation binding one generation to the next in a genealogy of spirit as well as of biology. In this sense when we acknowledge Jesus Christ as the head of the body we call the church, we affirm our unity with the imprint stamped upon a particular people by its various representative ancestors—Abraham and Sarah, Isaac and Rachael, David, Jeremiah, Mary, Joseph, and most significantly for us, Jesus Christ.

It is this view of the family that led St. Paul to declare that all who claim Jesus Christ as Lord are the descendents of Abraham. Those of us who are Gentile may not literally be of the household of Abraham and Sarah, but we bear the imprint of their faithfulness in our own lives. Consequently, for most of us, Abraham and Sarah are more than ancient figures in biblical history. Their faith is indelibly stamped into our perceptions and responses to life. We participate in their faith and their purposes. In the process our lives are permeated with their sense of responsibility to be the people of God wherever we may find ourselves.

It is in this view of the family that we discern one of the most basic insights into the Israelite conception of community. In this perspective children fulfill a function much more important than providing an emotional tie among family members across the generations or contributing to the economic well-being of the family. They are the bearers of the family name and heritage into the future. As such they introduce the values, customs, traditions, beliefs, and commitments received from their ancestors into the strange environments of the future. It is one of the continuing mysteries of God that the unity and mission of the people of God are dependent upon the faithfulness with which each generation of families accepts this task.

The Israelite conception of time was dynamic, not static. Children as bearers of culture into the future, therefore, not only were the vehicles whereby the meanings and customs of the past entered the future. They challenged and refined the purposes and practices inherited from the past as they adapted them to the requirements of each new situation. It is such a view that led the writer of Isaiah to envision that, in the fulfillment of the harmony of God's creation, a little child shall lead us all (Isaiah 11:6). It undergirds, moreover, the statement of Jesus that "whoever does not receive the kingdom of God like a child shall not enter it" (Mark 10:15, RSV).

Moses, Samuel, David, Jeremiah, and Jesus all come to mind as people whose childhood experiences and perceptions later contributed to their adult refinement of Israelite faith and life. If the stories had been told, similar childhood experiences undoubtedly shaped the contributions of Deborah, Hannah, Esther, and Mary to the life and faith of the larger community. In each case, they introduced into their experience of the contemporary age commitments and values received from the past, but with a sense of responsibility to the ever-present creative activity of God. In the process, their actions eventually disrupted some of the values and practices of those they loved. This experience is not an uncommon one. The birth of a child may be received as a gift, but each child has the potential to disrupt the expectations of those who love her or him. At times they become the bearers of a future we may not wish to see. And yet that future may be more attuned to the purposes of God than our own commitments and actions.

We have only to read the story of Samuel to be reminded that a child helped usher in a future filled with personal anguish for the elderly priest Eli, who had taken him into the love and care of his own household. We can see it in the anguish of David, whose sons disrupted not only his dreams for them but his dreams for the nation. We can hear it in Mary's confusion as she wondered why the young Jesus had remained behind to converse with the priests in the temple in Jerusalem, and in her grief as she stood with the disciple whom Jesus loved near the foot of the cross.

It is in the challenge children make to the culture they inherit that much pain is felt by an older generation—an experience most poignantly felt by many during the 1960s. But in that challenge, if the children are faithful to their heritage, they help illumine the values and meanings of the practices and commitments received from the past for what they are. The parochialism, idolatry, lack of compassion, and justice, and the faithlessness of their elders is unmasked; and the majesty and glory of God may be revealed for those with eyes to see and ears to hear.

In the simultaneous tasks of perpetuating the destiny of the family while also challenging many of its basic assumptions and practices, children also help recreate the community for an ever-changing present. The future is pregnant with the possibilities in the gift of each child to the community. Children are significant because they embody the community's trust in the future based on meanings drawn from its vision out of its corporate past. It is, after all, only as one is able to perceive life from the perspective of the child and to respond to it with the spontaneity and openness of the child that one can enter into the full range of life's meaning and possibilities. The kingdom of God is for children—children of all ages who recognize that in their dependence upon God they usher in a new age.

At this point, the biblical account is most difficult for the contemporary world citizen to comprehend. Our situation is quite different. Rather than having a shortage of children to carry what we value into the future, we have more children than we can adequately feed, clothe, or house. We do an even poorer job of preparing vast numbers of children to pick up the mantle of the future through effective educational programs, adequate health care, and a bountiful supply of nurturing relationships.

A growing number of people are admitting the very real interruptions children can make in their lives. They recognize the financial and emotional burdens children place on a family.

They acknowledge that children may not be all that cute or loveable. Consequently, more and more people are choosing not to have children. Still others, including many grandparents, choose to live in places and to participate in organizations that limit any interaction with children. Perhaps even more serious for the corporate life of the nation, these same people, often without realizing it, also make the decision to be "anti-children." Such a response may be seen in their refusal to vote for levies that support needed children's health, welfare, and educational services. They abdicate their responsibilities for assuming leadership roles with children's groups. They support housing patterns that discriminate against children—contributing to the creation of ghettos distinguished only by the absence or presence of children. They deny adequate support systems for the programs and resources needed for a viable ministry with children in many churches. And, perhaps most seriously, they lose the child's angle of vision on their own decisions and actions, and regard their own efforts with too much seriousness. Through such actions, this ever larger group of people in our society stands against the biblical perspective that the children in our midst are indeed the bearers of the culture into the future. Increasingly they deny the resources of the community needed by children to appropriate their heritage as the basis for responsible decisions regarding our corporate future.

Children Are Agents of God's Purposes

In the birth of a child, especially through the first-born son, the vision of the community that had dominated Israel's perception of its future destiny was renewed and revitalized. It was through the children of Isaac, and Isaac's grandchildren and great-grandchildren, that the covenant made between God and Abraham could be realized in a future time. As the bearers into the new age of the agreements made between God and their ancestors, the sons and daughters of Abraham and Sarah and all the other representative parents of the Israelite community extend the mission of God for yet another time and to yet another people. In the process, children are more than the bearers of Israelite culture, they convey the promises of the steadfast love of God into new situations, with new expectations and changing responsibilities. The presence of children is crucial, therefore, for they are the means of the continuance and extension of God's covenantal relationship with all peoples.

From such a perspective, children are more than the joy of their parents. They are more than a parent's security for old age. They provide more than pleasure for the present. They are a primary means of God's gracious activity. We must be careful, once again, that we not equate this biblical view with people who have not yet reached some culturally defined stage of maturity. Rather, we are reminded that, as the children of those who participate in the covenants of our ancestors, we participate in God's redemptive activity no matter what our age might be. God spoke through Samuel, a child, and used the boy with the lunch of bread and fish. God also spoke through the sons and daughters of Abraham and Sarah in one generation after another down through the centuries. Again, our relationship to the activity of God is perhaps most clearly seen in the redemptive work of Jesus Christ, *Son* of God. It was as God's Son that Jesus Christ revealed the love and will of God in his preaching, teaching, healing, and ultimately in his faithful walk to Golgotha. Similarly, when our own service reflects the trusting obedience of childlikeness, our work may embody God's purposes in this place and age.

One of the apparent contradictions of the biblical witness arises from the claim that children serve as agents of God's purposes by being models for our spiritual growth. Samuel Terrien has reminded us that childhood as a model is, at best, ambiguous, for "children are natural exemplars of egocentric irresponsibility. . . ."[10] Yet Jesus gathered the children around him, explaining to his disciples that they could not experience the richness and fullness of God's presence without becoming as little children. That is a hard saying for those of us who have passed the years of childhood. We tend to view the Christian life in adult terms, with adult categories, adult expectations, and adult behaviors. But Jesus clearly identified the child, in spite of the ambiguity exemplified in this small re-presentation of God's creative spirit, as an important model for our own spiritual existence.

Terrien, quoting Francis Thompson, notes that a child is quite different from an adult. A child sees "a world in a grain of sand, and an eternity in an hour." We often see sand as grit messing up the house and time as a frustrating set of limitations. Children do not look upon life as a sentence to be endured. Neither are they so tired of life that they desire it to be "commuted into death."[11] Instead, children know the limits of human knowledge without being confined by the boundaries of those limits. In fact, they are constantly pushing at those boundaries simply to discover how far they can be stretched.

Children know that the best of intentions may lead to disastrous consequences—a characteristic of childhood that is the creative underpinning for most cartoon strips featuring children. Who does not recognize the anticipation of Charlie Brown as he races to kick the football Lucy is holding? Who does not suffer with him the repeated anguish of failed trust? Who does not empathize with Dennis the Menace sitting in the corner after some highly anticipated but disastrous activity? Who does not hope with Peppermint Patti that just once in her continuing struggle with the school system, she might receive an "A"? In spite of the repeated setbacks they experience in their attempts to trust, to risk, and to hope, such children continue to recognize that the mystery, beauty, and joy somehow transcend the finitude, ignorance, injustice, hopelessness, and even the lack of love encountered in their relationships with others.

It is in their sense of the potential in the mundane that children most effectively help us see the glory of God revealed in the common and the ordinary—in a loaf of bread, the juice of the grape, the touch of a compassionate hand, a hug, a flower, a friendly and oft-repeated greeting. Such are the events of the kingdom of God. They are most readily available to those who experience life with the wide-eyed anticipation of children.

Children, as agents of God's purposes, are also capable of serving in the life and mission of the church. They remind us that people do not need to wait until reaching some magical age before they can engage in acts of love and justice. In accordance with our capacities any one of us may participate in God's creative and redemptive work in our contemporary world. Usually when we think of ways to implement the work of God, our thoughts turn to the designated offices of our religious institutions, or to those in roles of authority in our communities. As important as these offices and roles may be, they are only one way God works. Obviously they are not particularly appropriate for young people. Neither are they appropriate for the older person who has recently joined the community. Lacking knowledge of the community's heritage, experience in the daily affairs of the community, and skills in the manner of the community's ministry, such a person approaches the resources and the responsibilities of the community much like a child.

The ministries of the faith communities that children and newcomers may participate in with meaning and power may be specific activities. They may engage in ministries where the imprisoned are visited, the hungry are fed, the naked are clothed, and the sick are comforted. A young slave girl had the temerity to suggest that Naaman, counselor to the king of Syria, might seek healing from the prophet Elisha for his leprosy. The gospels tell of the young lad who readily contributed his five loaves and two fishes that the mulitudes might be fed. Similar small and specific actions not only made a difference in biblical times; they still do.

I am reminded of the boy who rode in the car with his mother while she drove some poor and elderly people to the grocery store or medical offices. As much as each person appreciated the service, most looked forward even more to the bright spot that child's presence brought to their days. A simple illustration perhaps, but a significant example of the ministries of children and other childlike persons.

Unfortunately, the potential young children have to serve as

God's agents for the whole community is often inhibited by the peer-group structures we have created for them. We isolate them in special structures for education and socialization. Many local churches further segregate their worship life and missional efforts along the lines of age groups. Children are thereby isolated from the primary acts and relationships of congregational celebration and service. These divisions may make the administration of congregational life more manageable. They undermine, however, the corporate character of the church as the body of Christ and diminish the interdependence of the ministries of all people in the church.

Children do minister. Dennis Benson and Stan Stewart, through their popular little book on *The Ministry of the Child,* repeatedly illustrate this fact. Children often perceive truth where more sophisticated adults see only confusion. They can effect reconciliation in the midst of conflict and tension. They are able to comfort the sick and to warm the hearts of the lonely. They may bring a sense of hope to the despondent and despairing. They have, in other words, the capacity to serve as God's agents at the many points where our deepest needs are expressed. Children not only need the church, but "the church desperately needs the children." Not only does it need the explicit ministries of children, it needs what Benson and Stuart have called the openness characteristic of the "child spirit" in people of all ages.[12] The economy of God's creation is once again evident in the mutuality of the faith responses of children and adults. Both are crucial in conveying the good news of God's redeeming love to all humanity.

Summary
Deeply rooted in our biblical heritage is the conviction that all of us live as children of God. No matter what our age, we relate to our Creator as no more and no less than children. In the birth and rebirth of people, we receive the ever-new and yet ever-present creative spirit of God as a gift. This gift is not one we can possess or claim for ourselves alone. The new life in our midst is a gift for the sake of the whole community. Those who

enter our midst appropriate the resources of our corporate heritage and extend the distinctive character of our cultural life into the future. As they take on the values, customs, and commitments received from the past, they also hand them on. Children are consequently the obvious link between past and future. Through them we experience not only the continuity of the race but the ever-present reality of God's covenantal love. Children, however, do not engage in this process of transmission passively. Even as they have been influenced and shaped by the content of their heritage, they adapt, modify, and alter it for the future. In so doing, they may act as the agents of God's continuing creative power in our midst. Through them the resurging visions of peace and justice are kindled anew. Children of all ages have a significant place and function in the order of creation.

CHAPTER 3

ON BEING CHILDLIKE
A Biblical Perspective

When I was a child, my speech, my outlook, and my
thoughts were all childish. When I grew up, I had
finished with childish things. Now we see only puzzling
reflections in a mirror, but then we shall see face to
face. My knowledge now is partial; then it will be
whole, like God's knowledge of me. (I Cor. 13:11-12,
NEB)

"Let the children come to me; do not try to stop
them; for the kingdom of God belongs to such as these.
I tell you, whoever does not accept the kingdom of God
like a child will never enter it." (Mark 10:14-15, NEB)

When we begin with the theological premise that all of us,
despite our differences in age, are children of God, the
distinctions we usually make along age lines to describe
maturity must be reviewed. This is not to say that the variations
in the capacities and abilities between birth and death are not
important. It is to emphasize certain commonalities in the
human experience throughout the life cycle. Among these
commonalities is the recurring interplay between certain events
that make possible new meanings for our lives and those that
incorporate and integrate new experiences into older meanings. The former, while most visible in the lives of children as

they encounter new information and make new discoveries, may continue throughout adulthood. The latter, while usually associated with the responses of adults in the middle to late stages of the life cycle, may nevertheless be found in the lives of children as they organize their experiences into some comprehensible whole. This interplay characterizes the dynamics of our faith pilgrimages as well. The events and circumstances of life never cease to keep us torn between the temptation to respond to them with the faith of children and the desire to respond to them with a childlike faith. In the pages that follow, I intend to explore this lifelong rhythmic pattern of being open to the new and integrating the subsequent experience into previously existing faith commitments and meanings. It is my contention that the specific content of our personal identities is grounded in, and emerges from, these commitments—a second emphasis of this chapter. I will then identify several tasks central to our pilgrimages of faith and some clues for the quality of faith found in the maturity of childlikeness.

Undifferentiated to Differentiated Faith

One of many strange statements to be found in the teachings of Jesus occurs in all three of the Synoptic Gospels (Mark 10:13-16, Luke 18:15-17, Matt. 18:1-4). The situation was not an uncommon one. People had gathered to hear Jesus teach. A number of children may have squeezed their way through the adult crowd so that they could sit on the front row, perhaps at the feet of Jesus. The disciples intervened, leading the children away from the center of the crowd. Jesus stopped them, called the children back to him and blessed them. He then spoke to the crowd, saying that, unless they became as little children they would not enter the kingdom of heaven.

Through this little encounter, another of the paradoxes of discipleship is identified. An important clue to the life of faith is to be found in certain qualities of childlikeness. Jesus obviously did not intend to encourage us to remain in a state of childhood. At no point did Jesus or his followers make the *experience* of children a model for the faithful life. On the contrary, Paul in his letter to the Corinthians makes it quite clear that maturity of faith is not to be found in perpetuating childish attitudes or behavior. Rather, our speech, feelings, and thoughts are to be those of an adult (I Cor. 13:11).

These two passages are not contradictory. They convey a picture of the life of faith from two different angles of vision. In the Gospel accounts we are confronted in Jesus' words with the tendency among adults to divorce their responses to God from the resources of childhood. This view, held perhaps by the disciples and certainly by many today, looks upon children as not yet ready to appreciate or to respond to the initiative of God in and through the life of the community. On the other hand, Jesus' words counter the popular conception that, to be faithful adults, we must repress, or at least outgrow, the child's patterns of responding to the mysteries of life. In either case, such a faith lacks both depth and spontaneity.

The statement of Paul reflects an opposite concern. Reviewing the rivalry, conflicts, self-centeredness, and pettiness of the Corinthian congregation, he reminds its members that the faith of adults is not to be marred by arrested patterns of childhood. On the contrary, Paul observes that the process of maturing faith may be compared to the emerging reflection we see of ourselves in a mirror. Paul, of course, was not referring to our clear, silver-backed glass mirrors. He had in mind the highly polished metal mirrors commonly used in the first century. The images we see in contemporary mirrors are clear and contain few distortions. But the brass and silver mirrors of ancient Corinth lacked that clarity. An initial glance would, according to Moffat, produce only "baffling reflections." The New English Bible describes the same image as "puzzling reflections." With good light, a person might see a reflection sharply—"face to face"—as Paul observes. With this common experience before his reader, Paul tells his friends in Corinth, and reminds us as well, that with growing wisdom and maturity, we might eventually see and know ourselves as we are seen and known by God—a clarity heretofore known only to God.

The discovery of an undeveloped and forgotten roll of film in the back corner of a desk drawer may lead us to an experience similar to that described by Paul. If we were to develop it ourselves, our first impression would be that of undifferentiated darkness. However, once it has been put in the developing solution, lines and shaded figures would soon begin to appear. At first we might well be puzzled. We would not be able to tell who or what the picture is about. But as the process continues, the lines and figures would become increasingly evident, until, face to face, we would encounter our own reflection.

Were we to think about the picture for a few minutes, several things would undoubtedly soon happen. 1) We would see our image distinctly and clearly. 2) What was in the total picture would enable us to remember where we were and what we were doing when it was taken. 3) It would also enable us to identify other people who, for a time at least, linked us with the total human experience. 4) It would trigger memories of a given event or relationship and the meanings clustered around them. We would begin to see ourselves in that context. We would recall some of our commitments and what gave our lives meaning at that time. In short, we would be able to reconstruct that moment in the context of our lives.

Faith in Life's Pilgrimage

The image of seeing ourselves first dimly and then gradually face to face may provide a clue into the dynamics of another metaphor for the journey through life from birth to death. The pilgrimage gathers up much of the experience I have been describing. It is common to all. It may take many forms. Each entails movement, however, from a condition in which it is hard to discern who we are or what we are about to one in which we can see the way we relate to our physical and historical context with greater clarity. It conveys a sense of moving out, a leaving, a going, as well as a coming and resting. It underscores the changes in life. A pilgrimage historically did not involve the simple task of climbing aboard an airplane for a distant shrine. It did not entail traversing the shortest distance between two places. In no way could it be described in a linear or sequential fashion. Life as a pilgrimage does not necessarily involve the steady progression from one stage or place to another until our destination is finally reached. Even though the graded and sequential structures of our schools and church schools tend to follow this assumption, too many temptations and comfortable way stations intrude upon the natural processes of growth to allow us to fall into such simplistic thinking. A pilgrimage involves specific experiences and disciplines that bring into focus the meaning and purpose of one's life much as the developing processes bring the photographic image into focus. One can never cease in the quest to clarify the center of one's loyalty and devotion until death intervenes.[1]

A pilgrimage may take many forms. It often follows a planned route with way stations for rest and renewal along the way. It may be an exodus—an abrupt dislocation from the comforts of home into the uncharted paths of some wilderness in the search for a promised land. It may be captivity and exile in a strange country filled with alien gods and unfamiliar customs and expectations. It may be a "flight into Egypt" to escape certain death and destruction of body, mind, or spirit.

Whatever the form of our journey to increased self-awareness and purpose, we find our meanings and our identity in the fusion of ourselves with the people around us, in the heritage they embody, and in the place in which we live. This undifferentiated perspective is characteristic of the responses of young children to life. In his discussion of the faith characteristics of people throughout life, John Westerhoff has observed that young children participate in the faith of their elders and significant others. He calls this faith response an "experienced faith."[2] It is enactive in the sense that the faith of children is organized around what can be seen, touched, and heard. Order and purpose emerge as they make connections between what they can see, touch, smell, and physically manipulate. But their faith as "experienced" is even more deeply connected to those who nurture them. Children are clearly not extensions of their parents. They have distinct personalities. Yet the context that gives that identity its content is clearly shaped by the omniscience and omnipresence of parents and significant others. In this sense the identity of young children is relatively undifferentiated from that of their parents. The custom of calling a child "the Jones's boy" or "the Garcia's daughter" may point to the way the relationship child to parent is described in our daily conversation. The insistent "no" of the "terrible" two-year-old is a crucial step in the development of personal identity, as Erik Erikson has emphasized. But those often painful moments when child opposes parent only reflect the extent to which the child's sense of identity is grounded in the experience and commitments of the parents. The importance of these moments of grounding in the faith of our parents cannot be underestimated. It is through those relationships that the nuances of the historical sources of the faith of the community are passed on from one person to another and from one generation to the next.

Metaphorically speaking, young children cannot distinguish themselves in a mirror of reflections. Instead, the image is puzzling or baffling to them. Such is the character of our own first steps into life. It also may describe our experience at any age, as we enter any radically new experience or move through a major rite of passage. Whether we are young or old, we enter that experience through our identification with some significant others. The five-year-old child tightly grips the security and strength of her mother as they enter the school hand-in-hand on the first day of class. Through the vision the mother has of the significance of the school for her daughter and the protective shield she provides by her presence, the child encounters that experience—not alone, but with the power and security of that larger other. The trust the Hebrews placed in Moses to lead them out of the "job security" of their slavery into the unknown wilderness illustrates a similar phenomenon among adults. So did the willingness of many black and white Americans to entrust themselves to the vision and strategies of Martin Luther King, Jr., and his colleagues. And so does my own cautious habit of watching the leaders of a group I am attending for the first time for clues regarding what is expected of those present so that I will not feel like a stranger or do something considered inappropriate. The fact that the unknown pains of school, wilderness, or freedom march are, for many, more intolerable than the known pains of remaining in the undifferentiated conditions of being children, slaves, or second-class citizens should not surprise us. Such people, at the time at least, do not want to see more clearly. They would rather perpetuate their identities as defined by their parents, slaveholders, or "first-class citizens."

Self-Awareness in Life's Pilgrimage

The movement I am describing, in our faith/identity pilgrimage from puzzling reflections to face-to-face self-awareness, Carl Jung called the process of differentiation. The process of differentiation is not unlike that described by Paul in I Corinthians. Initially, as infants just born into the community, as newcomers still trying to make sense out of the language, patterns of relationships, values, and attitudes in a new community, or as people acquiring a new role or status involving new expectations and responsibilities in the community, we participate in the images, symbols, and meanings surrounding us, unaware of their existence. We simply do not make distinctions among these resources of the community's heritage. Some take precedence in our life because of the significance they have for those who surround us, or through the power of their immediacy to us. As we move from one experience to another, we may gradually begin to make distinctions among the many impressions we receive.

The process is familiar to all of us in the cognitive efforts young children make to put words to their experience. At first, *doggie* may describe any soft and fuzzy creature. A cat is a *doggie*. So are cows, bears, even chickens and ducks. With additional experience and more discrete information the child makes the distinction between a dog and a cat. Gradually, more and more varieties of animals are added to his or her perception of the world. The child gradually differentiates the animal kingdom. A similar process occurs with other objects that may be seen, heard, and touched. It takes place whenever we move into a new situation or place and are at first unclear about what behavior is considered acceptable or unacceptable. It is evident in the first weeks after young parents bring home their first child. At first, all cries sound alike. Later they can tell which are hungry, angry, or attention-seeking cries. Differention may be seen in the movement many people make from vague or general commitments to specific and purposeful commitments. The process of making distinctions, in other words, is evident in our relationship both to those things available to our senses and to those things we perceive abstractly.

Perhaps the latter is evident in the approach many take to the biblical record. For some, the Bible is the undifferentiated word of God. They often do not perceive the differences, for example, in the way the ancient writers of Genesis, the priestly writers of the kingdom of Israel, or the prophets understood the way God works in human history; or the changes evident in the way Israel approached her mission to the nations. These distinctions are glossed over in simplistic claims, similar to the child's view that any four-legged animal is a "doggie." The ability to distinguish, in other words, is not only a matter of intellectual capacity. It has to do in part with the depth of our familiarity with the things, people, and events we encounter.

I am reminded of a young woman who, in the midst of a teacher-training event, came face-to-face with the fact that her faith commitments were not her own. She still participated, in a relatively unreflective way, in the faith of her parents and the older members of the small congregation in which she grew up. As she returned to the sessions of the class, her pain and discomfort intensified. Words that she thought had meaning in the past now seemed empty. Discrepancies between her beliefs and those of her elders became increasingly apparent. Indeed, some of the differences in the faith of her elders also became increasingly evident to her. The experience proved to be unsettling, even threatening to her. She felt at odds with the community that had nurtured her. In this situation, the people of that congregation also felt uncomfortable with the questions she was asking. To return to our mirror image for a moment, this young woman began to see herself with increasing clarity. Her own faith was beginning to emerge from the beliefs and values of those who had nurtured her. She began to discern some of the differences in her relationships with those in the congregation, and to recall the distinctive contribution each had made to her during her own faith pilgrimage. The unsettling process of making distinctions, in other words, is characteristic of our faith pilgrimages as well. It often involves pain and discomfort, but just as often it may include joy and celebration.

The Interdependence of Faith and Identity

At this point it may be important to recall our discussion in the first chapter regarding the nature of community. We live in community. It provides the framework for our living. It feeds the wellsprings of our imagination from the depths of its stories and traditions, rituals and symbols. It focuses our actions through its customs and rules. It nurtures us in the network of its relationships. It lends continuity to our lives through its institutions and structures. It transforms and energizes us through its celebrations. The content and structure of community, in other words, establish the boundaries and provide the resources for our pilgrimage—from the recurring, puzzling reflections of unexamined participation in life, to our face-to-face encounter with the depths of our experience reflected in maturity. During that journey we may transcend, or move beyond, the boundaries of given entities—whether of family, town, church, or nation. We may discover significant resources for our journeys in other finite expressions of the corporate experience of humanity. Hence these actions only widen the angle of our consciousness and expand our awareness of the vastness of the human community. Our emerging consciousness, in other words, is always grounded in a dynamic experience of community.

Perhaps the emerging mirror image of the photograph

described earlier may again be illustrative. The processes of differentiation involve our seeing ourselves ever more clearly in context. As we begin to discern our own image more clearly, the images around us also begin to take shape, and our relationship to our surroundings becomes increasingly apparent. The larger picture may reveal who was with us, what we were doing, where we were and the time in our lives when the event occurred. As we reflect on these obvious features, they evoke memories and stories about the people involved, the activity, the place, and some of the changes that have taken place in the interim. Further reflections may lead us into consideration of similar events and circumstances in our lives, in the lives of our children, and in the lives of our ancestors. They may even precipitate a discussion on some major social issue in the distant past when the picture was taken, in the present, or for the future.

An old photograph at a family reunion, a picture of army buddies, or a nostalgic visit with classmates pictured in the school yearbook often provide the occasion for reminiscences and reflections running the gamut of these topics. The resulting conversations may enable us to see ourselves in clearer perspective. They may recall and clarify our relationships to given people, certain places, and the flow of events in history. As we become increasingly conscious of who we were in that context, we become sensitive to similarities and differences in the values and commitments we shared with others then, and those that guide our decisions and actions now.

Seeing ourselves in context is not only integral to our sense of identity, it also lies at the heart of our faith commitments, a point Robert McAfee Brown's discussion of the nature of faith makes clear. In a summary of the many ways the word "faith" is used, both on the street and in theological discussions, he observes that each perspective refers to the way we make use of some past event or cluster of events to clarify or make sense out of our present situation. The content of the specific faith that serves as the organizing center for our lives, says Brown, has to do with 1) the event or events we appropriate to shape our perceptions of life, 2) the extent to which we allow the potential meanings and implications related to that event to inform our decisions in life, and 3) the nature and depth of our commitments to those meanings—i.e., our readiness to allow them to influence our actions and attitudes in life.[3] Our faith commitments consequently serve to inform us who we are, what we are to do, and why we believe it is important to engage in life's activities as we do. We may thus discern the interdependence of faith and identity in our life pilgrimages from an undifferentiated, to a differentiated awareness of our participation in the life of the community. Our commitments distinctively inform and shape our identities.

It is important to recall, however, that faith and identity are not achievements. Neither are they static. They do not follow any necessary sequential pattern in our lives. They are not fixed points in our experience. The interplay of ambiguity and clarity, of undifferentiated participation in, and differentiated engagement with, the community's events and meanings, continues throughout life. We see in the glass darkly—the experience of being a child in the community. Then in a moment of insight, we are conscious of our relationship to our context. We see clearly, face to face. We know ourselves as others know us. We then bump into a new situation or are caught up in changing circumstances, and we are again confronted with the dim glimmer of our reflection.

The interplay I have been describing characterizes the interdependence of faith and identity throughout our life pilgrimages. When we choose meanings and skills from all those available to us, we relate to certain past events in increasingly specific ways. They do not necessarily increase our estimation of our individuality, but they do increase our awareness of our identification with the whole human family. In the process we are confronted with the limits of being human. At the same time, we are humbled by the humanness of our limits. We discover, often to our dismay, that our commitments are not infinite, and neither are we. Yet we also discern the necessity of our making commitments if we are to draw upon the vast resources available to us from our corporate past. The Christ event becomes lively for us in our choosing to accept its claim upon our lives as the originating event for our living, just as the Exodus has been a lively event for Jews and many American blacks.

Commitment and the Integration of Faith and Identity

The awareness of our own finitude and consequent limitations in the choices at the center of our commitments allow us to appreciate the God-givenness of other faiths. We have the freedom to appreciate the gifts of God's presence through the commitments of those who order their lives around different events from the past, or even alternative perspectives on the same event. It does not free us, as Brown has recognized, from the necessity of making commitments. Rather, it frees us to make commitments that may empower us to be the bearers of the meanings from the past into the future.

Such an approach to life Westerhoff has described as "owned" faith.[4] Such a perspective implies that people are conscious of the commitments they make. They can appreciate the care and concern of the groups that have nurtured them, without being confined by their precepts and values. They have committed themselves to the possibilities of some past event for the future, without being overburdened by the ambiguous responses of those down through history who claimed a similar allegiance. They encounter life with courage drawn from that commitment, despite the despair they may experience in the trials and tribulations of simply living in a tormented and fractured world.[5] They witness to the potential of the power of that event to give meaning to the lives of others.

The extent of their commitment—the extent to which they "own" that past event, becomes the content of their faith. In the process, it reveals who they are in face-to-face encounters. They see themselves as participants in history—as recipients of the past and shapers of the future. They also see themselves incarnating the meanings of the past in the present. In their identification with the meanings of that event, their identities are revealed. They come to know themselves as they are already known.

These interplays throughout life shift people's relationship to their social and historical contexts. The process of differentiation expands our awareness of the immediate environment in which we find ourselves. We discover the hidden resources surrounding us. The process of integration, on the other hand, focuses that awareness in commitments to some of the meanings, values, and behaviors available to us in our larger social and historical contexts. We choose to live as Methodists or Presbyterians, citizens with a regional or international vision, with pro- or antiabortion beliefs. The integration of commitments is reflected in the consistency of values seen in the specific choices we make. Some event in the past, such as the Christ event, has the power to inform all that we do and consequently the power to give form to our lives. It reveals who we are. It functions as the organizing center for our living and doing. It serves as our springboard into the future—into what we may become.[6] And it frees us to live unfettered by contemporary events and circumstances. The image at this point is in focus. We see ourselves clearly—face to face. We are integrated beings, in unity with ourselves and our heritage.

In choosing such events from the past that may function normatively for our lives, at least four tasks are recurrently significant. They are present in a relatively unconscious form during childhood. They become increasingly evident whenever we engage in quests to comprehend the content of our affiliations, or when we enter into commitments that compel us to reorder our perceptions and actions. These tasks are central to any teaching or pastoral activity in the church.

Faith Identity Tasks: Making Space Sacred

The first task establishes the physical context for understanding who we are by *investing places with sacred meanings*. The continuing interdependent quest of the Hebrews to clarify their relationship to God as the Chosen People and to the Promised Land as their homeland illustrates the corporate character of this task. Sacred space—whether it be enclosed in a building or by given geographical features—designates the corporate identity of those who claim a special relationship to it. Important features distinguishing the folk at Christ Church from those who belong to St. John's are the altars in the buildings around which each respective group gathers. Similarly, the altars at Shechem, Bethel, and later, Jerusalem served as rallying points for the sons and daughters of Jacob. Geographic boundaries clarify the corporate identities of national groups, and capitol cities provide organizing centers for common alliances and loyalty. The interdependence of identity and place is reflected in our Pledge of Allegiance and in the rhetoric of our civic leaders, who evoke our common commitments by appealing to "we, the people of the United States . . . ." Consequently, not only rivers and mountain ridges, but imaginary lines through deserts have been defended down through the ages as the borders demarking "our collective space." Transgressions into that space arouse intense and often hostile feelings because they represent a threat to our corporate self-understanding.

The task of making space sacred takes at least three forms during our faith journeys. In the first place *we endow the space around us with sacred meanings*. The reverence with which many view the places of their birth illustrates my point. It is evident in the sometimes irrational appeal of the homeland for the immigrant or refugee. Its lasting hold on many people may be seen in their desire to return to the places of their origin during the final years of their lives. The cycle from birth through life to death is thereby experienced as complete because one has returned to the place where one's life originated.

The process of endowing space with sacred meanings begins long before we are conscious of it. The space that surrounds us establishes the context for what and how we perceive and respond to subsequent events throughout our lives. The stories of the events of those places nurture our imaginations. Our work in those places shapes our expectations of what we can do. This point became evident to me when I tried to raise a garden in the Midwest according to the largely unconscious principles I had acquired as a child helping my father garden in the Pacific Northwest. It did not occur to me, for example, that my garden might need to be watered after a heavy rainstorm. But I had not reckoned with the fact that most of the downpour of midwestern summer rains runs off the top of the heavy clay soil, in contrast to the way Oregon's gentler rains had soaked into the sandy soil of my father's garden. Little water, consequently, reached the roots of my flowers and vegetables. Similar discoveries have been at the source of intense feelings of disorientation and dislocation of immigrant peoples in this land. The children of immigrants, however, are natives to the new place. They experience it as home, as Margaret Mead in *Culture and Commitment* and Oscar Handlin in *The Uprooted* have illustrated. It is the place of their origin. They are more comfortable with their surroundings because they are at least familiar with them. Their perceptions are shaped by their unconscious impressions of the place. They are unhampered by expectations acquired in another place, and consequently face the future grounded in the possibilities and limits of the place that has nurtured them. They endow that place, in other words, with sacred meanings.

As we continue our journeys of faith, we may move from the relatively unconscious task of endowing space with sacred meanings to *creating sacred places*. This process also begins at a very early age. Young children, for example, often find a special corner for play. It may be the space behind the bed, under the stairs or in an appliance box. Much time and energy is spent in decorating and arranging belongings in the space. They may spend hours alone in that place. They are often ready and willing to let others see and admire it, but do not allow others to alter it. Many parents have not understood the traumatic consequences of their efforts to clean up the places where their children play. In their moving and reordering of toys and playthings, they have invaded the turf of their children and upset the sacred order of the worlds they have been creating. Children are not alone in wanting to preserve the sacred order they have created in their small corners of the world. Many adults do not want anyone to alter the piles of papers and books on their desks, to rearrange the dishes in the kitchen cupboard, or to move any tools from their designated places in the shop.

The task of creating sacred spaces occurs not only at the private level of our existence—it consumes our corporate energies as well. We build churches, shrines, memorials, and cemeteries. We establish zoning laws, school districts, towns, and cities. We designate certain parts of our land to be set aside as parks and wilderness areas. In each case we choose to "set aside" given segments of our common land for special purposes. We endow them with special meanings. And we often relate to them with special rituals. We write songs to capture their meanings for us. We develop codes of conduct to guide our behavior in the use of those places. They are special places in our common lives.

As people move on in their pilgrimages of faith, *they begin to relate to all of creation as sacred.* This does not happen in a generalized manner. Rather, in appropriating the meanings clustered around a given place, some people are able to discern its connection to the whole of creation. They perceive the whole world in a grain of sand. They experience any place as the Promised Land. The Kingdom of God does not exist for them in the future. It is at hand. The vision such people have of life encompasses the whole of creation.

The identity of such people is not diffuse and general. They are not "all things to all people." On the contrary, their commitments may be very specific, and their physical ties to the world may be quite limited. Their perception of life's meanings, however, is not confined by the limits of their experience or the boundaries of any given territory. John Wesley reflected the spirit of such a person in observing that all the world was his parish. So does Mother Teresa, who sees the future of the race in a starving child in Calcutta. Such people affirm the unity of the world in spite of our human divisions. They honor the interdependence of all people as the children of God. They see the glory and majesty of creation revealed in a leaf, a child, a brook, an aging adult. They see all creation as the kingdom of God. Their primary allegiance as citizens is to the created order as defined by God and not to the divisions we human beings have constructed.

The interplay of tasks, from endowing given places with sacred meanings to discerning the sacred in all of creation, consumes much of our time and energy during our faith journeys. The energy and effort the Hebrews expended to keep the ark of the covenant with them throughout their sojourn in the desert may illustrate my point. This symbol of their corporate identity had to be approached respectfully and treated with great care. Rituals to preserve and perpetuate its sacred place in their life provided a purpose and security for their comings and goings. We may see a similar, albeit much less profound, attempt to sanctify the temporary places we visit in our own traveling. Among the first things many of us do after checking into a hotel or motel is unpack our suitcases, put our belongings away, and arrange the room so that we will be comfortable. We seek, even in a minimal way, to render the strange place hospitable.

The task of endowing space with sacred meanings involves more than establishing the familiar in the new places in which we find ourselves. Unexpected events and new circumstances continually alter our relationship to our surroundings, sometimes as subtly as through the arrival of a new family on the block, or as dramatically as by the destruction of a tornado. *We consequently experience dislocation—a sense of being in a strange place.* The house next door is not the same place with new occupants. The street is alien without the great oak tree on the corner. Such dislocation confronts us with the necessity of establishing a new relationship to once-familiar territory. It provides us with a new occasion to expand and/or integrate meanings we have brought with us to this point in our lives.

The sources of such dislocation are many. They may entail the struggle of entering some new phase in our own physical, moral, or intellectual development. They may have been precipitated by some new role or status in the community. They may have been caused by social, political, or economic changes over which we have no control. The experience, whatever the cause, is one of exodus or exile. We are no longer secure with our knowledge of our surroundings.

In the experience of dislocation, we often yield to the temptation to limit our awareness of the sacred and holy to specific places. We often end up sidetracked on our journeys and spend our time wandering in the desolate quest for familiar signs of the sacred. We may retreat to the familiarity and security of places we have previously known. At the same time, we often long for a Moses to show us the way and to confirm for us that God is in our midst. But we may also settle gratefully for the Aarons who create golden calves to give us the feeling that their presence can make any place special. In spite of our experiences of dislocation, there is always the possibility that we will discover again a sense of vision and purpose. When that occurs, we then understand personally the fear, wonder and joy the Hebrews felt when Moses returned with the stone tablets. Like them, we may be emboldened to destroy the idols we have created in the meantime, to clarify our commitments once again, and to renew our pilgrimages of faith, affiirming that we live in the grace of God no matter how strange our surroundings.

Faith Identity Task: Making Sense of Time

A second task for establishing the context for understanding who we are involves locating ourselves in the flow of temporal meanings. Specifically this aspect of our faith journeys entails (in Robert McAfee Brown's words), "the creative appropriation of an open past."[7] The process is not unfamiliar to us. Perhaps Alex Haley, most recently through his quest for his own roots, has made us conscious of the way our investigations into our personal and corporate pasts not only open up meanings hidden from us, but possibilities heretofore unknown to us. Certainly Haley inspired a host of other Americans to visit cemeteries, genealogical collections, and historical libraries in search of ancestral information. Those efforts often illumined the continuities of current and past values and behaviors. They uncovered incidents revealing the character of those who nurtured their parents and grandparents. These investigations made available to a present generation the commitments leading certain ancestors to take great risks for the future of their families and loved ones. This quest, in other words, has helped open up meanings in experiences hidden from our view, but still influential in shaping who we are.

The power in past events arises, as Brown points out, from what we do with the past. Since the past can never be perfectly repeated, we must always make some decision about what to do with it. Our options are many. We can allow the past to haunt our imaginations or plague our consciences. We may seek to rectify the past, to honor or celebrate it. I am reminded of a friend, a staunch civil rights activist during the 1960s, who discovered that some of his ancestors had owned slaves. This discovery shocked him. Unable to ignore that information, he then had to choose what to do with it. That past was abhorrent to him, yet it confronted him with the realization that he, too, had shared in the collective experience of slaveholding. At its most basic level was the fact that several inherited antiques in his home had originally been purchased by the sweat of slave labor. He chose to appropriate the meanings of that event by accepting his complicity in the evils of a socially, culturally, economically, and religiously segregated society. That decision changed the way he related, not only to those who tried to preserve patterns of white supremacy, but also to those seeking equal access to the rights and privileges of a democratic society.

Faith, Brown reiterates, involves not only the creative appropriation of an open past, but is also evident in the "dynamic interrelationships" of the content we perceive in those events and our commitments to them.[8] Their significance for our lives is determined by the "degree of commitment" we make to their content.[9] My friend's discovery altered the nature of his response to civil rights issues. It did not make him less active. It made him more sensitive to the pain of all parties. It transformed his involvement from a rational concern for the rights of the disenfranchised into a deeply personal commitment to the needs of all people for healing and reconciliation. It intensified his commitment.

When we commit ourselves to the content of certain past events, the relationship of our faith and our identity may be made evident. Again Brown's discussion is useful. He develops four cumulative theses that illuminate this interdependence. In the first, he notes that *"certain events from the past are normative for us, defining who we are."*[10] Some events, such as the day of our birth, are determined for us. Consequently, we become children of the Depression, of the Great War, or of the Vietnam era by virtue of that fact. Being surrounded by those events during our early years significantly influences our perceptions and expectations—as may be seen in the conflict of values between many parents who lived through the Depression and their children who grew up surrounded by the indulgence of the 1950s.

Other events, however, we choose as being significant for understanding who we are. Among the numerous faith options available to us, those of us who choose to relate ourselves to the Christ event, for example, identify ourselves as contemporary bearers of its meanings. We assume the name "Christian" and seek to measure the way we live against our understanding of what is expected of those who attempt to introduce the meanings of that event into our contemporary age. In this sense, the Christ event becomes normative for us, defining who we are.

Second, *we consciously choose to relate "to certain events from the past in ways that help them give meaning to who we are and what we do."* They have "revelatory significance for us."[11] They illuminate what we are doing and what we might do. We make use of the past to shed light on the present and future. It informs how we choose to act and to relate to the people and to the circumstances in which we now find ourselves. The exodus has served as such a revelatory event for many black American

Christians. The common experience of bondage, the sense of peoplehood, and the vision of a promised land transcended the differences of slavery in the "brickyards" of Egypt, to use Walter Brueggeman's image,[12] and the cotton plantations of the American South. That ancient event provided a way of seeing through their contemporary experience. It provided the basis for personal and corporate pride that could not be undermined by the degradation of slavery. It filled them with hope in spite of the despair they knew in their daily routines. It provided them with a way to see meaning in the horror of their lot in life. Such is the potential power in those events we choose as normative for our lives.

Third, *"we shape our lives in conformity to the meaning of those events.* They become occasions of power as well as wisdom. They not only reveal to us who we have been; they also challenge us to be transformed into what we can become."[13] They hold up a model, a guide or example for our lives. They call us to explore the depth of the potential in our capacities and to test the limits of our abilities. They place expectations upon our responses to contemporary events and measure the extent to which our commitments are faithful to those who nurtured us. Many of our prayers and hymns illustrate this phenomenon. They evoke the lively concern of people to conform their lives to that of Jesus Christ. Paul would claim, for example, that he was a servant of Jesus Christ. St. Francis, in seeking to emulate his master, gave up everything to trust in the providence of God with the same sense of expectant dependence found in the sparrows, in the lilies, and in children. Teachers in church schools have urged young people to follow the example of Jesus in the songs they choose to sing ("Lord, We Are Able to Be Crucified with Thee") or the values they uphold ("Love Your Neighbors As Yourself"). In each case, these people understood that our identities are to be found in the extent to which we commit ourselves.

In the fourth place Brown observes that *"conformity to normative events of the past is not bondage but liberation.* It is characteristically by our surrender to them that we are truly freed for the present and the future."[14] George Mattheson, a nineteenth-century Scottish pastor, acknowledged the same insight in the words of a familiar hymn, "Make me a captive, Lord, and then I shall be free."

We do not approach the conflicting demands of each day empty and without form. The content of our commitments defines who we are in the confusion of the many conflicting demands on our time and energy. It provides clues for our decisions about the way we handle the routine chores of our lives. It gives us a sense of direction. It frees us from the confinement of an eternal present by reminding us of the heritage that has nurtured us and envisioning a future for us that fulfills hopes received through our common heritage.

The process of choosing events from the past continues throughout our lives. For young children, those events are most clearly related to their immediate experience. As we mature in years, we have the growing capacity to relate to the meanings of events that are increasingly distant from our experience. At its deepest level, we also have the capacity to discern possibilities for who we are in events that become paradigms for the deepest meanings in human existence. In choosing to relate to the symbolic as contrasted with the literal meanings of such events (creation, exodus, exile, incarnation), some people discern the interdependence of people across the more traditional lines of religion, culture, and nation that divide us. The power of such events is not derived from what actually happened in some clearly historical sense, but from the potential of what could happen in some symbolic sense.

The process, in whatever form, is continually threatened, however, by the intrusion of contemporary events into the flow of our lives. They often leave us confused. We may experience these intrusions as crises. They obscure details we once knew. They demand our immediate attention and distract our energies.

The result, in any case, *is a sense of disorientation.* We seem to be disconnected from meanings and commitments that once had power for our lives but have become impotent or lifeless.

Such an experience confronts us with the challenge once again to expand our consciousness, either by committing ourselves to another originating event, or by altering the way we have related to the one that has served as the center of our being. The risk of that commitment renews the momentum of our journey. It expands the options available to us. It clarifies anew a sense of direction. In the process, it further illuminates who we are and what we are about.

Faith Identity Task: Acknowledging Our Shadows

One of the most painful tasks in our pilgrimages centers on our repeated encounters with what Carl Jung has called the shadow in our lives. The shadow designates those possibilities in the human experience that we seek to avoid or reject. Since these possibilities always remain with us, we usually spend much time and energy trying to keep them from our conscious awareness. That task is not particularly difficult during the first half of our lives, because our shadows tend to remain below the surface of our consciousness.[15] But as we grow older, we have increasing difficulty avoiding their presence.

Flip Wilson, the comedian, has recently made us aware of the presence of the shadow in our lives in his famous response whenever he got caught in some disapproved action: "The devil made me do it." The "devil" exists in those repressed possibilities that intrude irrationally into our personal and corporate experience. They are evident in the contradictory practice of Christians who believed in the "fatherhood of God" and the "brotherhood of man" and continued to hold slaves. They account for the disparity between our words of concern for the poor and our political decisions denying the poor access to adequate health, housing, education, and jobs. They are reflected in our inability to see the hysteria of both protagonists and antagonists in any conflict—between two people or between nations. They are evident in the confusing behavior of parents who shower their children with affection one moment and beat them the next.

One of the most frightening tasks we undertake occurs when

we begin to encounter our personal and collective shadows face to face. In the fleeting moment of recognition of the evil and irrationality that exist in us, we are confronted with the realities of our finitude. We are forced to face the ambiguity of being human. We find it necessary to acknowledge our involvement in the destruction and suffering we knowingly and unknowingly have perpetuated. Such a task is threatening to the structures of our living. In a sense it calls for a conversion—a turning around to face ourselves with the knowledge that God has of us. It calls for an integration of ourselves as whole people—shadow and all.

One of the disturbing features of Jesus' ministry took place whenever and wherever he confronted people with their shadows. Many of the healing narratives conclude with the observation that the people were made "whole." The demons had been cast out and they had become integrated people. The same concern is evident in Jesus' encounter with the rich young man who had lived by the law but still felt alienated from life. Jesus quickly saw that his attachment to his wealth lurked beneath his conscious attempts to be faithful. The shadow is also evident in the continual bickering among the disciples regarding who among them was the greatest. Jesus responded to this concern by placing a child in their midst and confronting them with the discrepancy between their expectations and those of the one they followed.

The metaphor of the mirror image I have been using breaks down for us, however, in that the shadow is not passive. It can intrude into the carefully structured existence we have created for ourselves any time. The shadow can neither be absorbed nor abolished. We live in its presence at all times. The best that we can do is be conscious of its existence. Just as we may perceive the shadow on the wall behind us when we look closely in the mirror, conscious people will always be aware of its presence in their lives.

Accepting the continuing presence of the shadow of our consciousness involves living with the awareness that we are both rational and irrational, loving and unloving, just and unjust, responsible and irresponsible. It entails accepting the reality of our finitude. The consequence is again a paradox. In our awareness of the shadow of our consciousness, we gain a clearer sense of who we are than was previously possible. The shape of our personalities becomes increasingly distinct. We see ourselves more clearly. At the same time, our sense of communion with the whole of humanity becomes more intense. We see ourselves more clearly because we recognize ourselves in our human context. In choosing to confront the shadow of the self, we have chosen to be human and have rejected the very human tendency to view ourselves as godlike. We acknowledge our dependence, our status as children of the Creator. Perhaps of greatest significance, we have acknowledged that we will die.

When we refuse to acknowledge those latent possibilities lurking just beneath our awareness, our lives are dominated by baffling reflections of ourselves. We may speak, as Paul writes, "with the tongues of angels," but the resulting sound is flat and lifeless. We may present rational, orderly images of ourselves, but they are filled with illusions.

The intrusion of those possibilities from the shadow of our consciousness in our lives presents us with a new opportunity for clarifying who we are and what we are about. It confronts us, for the moment, with the possibility of knowing ourselves as we are known by God. When we accept that challenge, we continue our pilgrimage from the virtual absence of consciousness of our surroundings characteristic of children to a growing awareness of seeing ourselves face to face in the context of all creation.

Faith Identity Task:
Seeing the Image of God in Ourselves

A fourth task in our journeys of faith involves seeing the image of the Creator in ourselves. When we discover the imprint of God in our lives, we see ourselves fully and clearly. We usually call this task *religious*. It occurs as we recognize that we do not control our destinies, but live by the mercy of a transrational power that, although it exists beyond our consciousness, we nevertheless accept with humility. It is at this point, as Jacobi reminds us, that we allow ourselves to be conscious of our dependence upon that power, and recognize that our lives are measured against the one we call God and all creation, and not by some human measure.[16]

This knowledge confronts us with our interdependence with the total human family. We do not stand alone or against each other. Quite the contrary; we all trace our existence to the act of creation and to God, the source of all things. We live, not by the efforts of our own will, but through the grace and mercy of the One who sustains all of life. We live, not by our own imagination and initiative, but in the bounty of the providence of God. In coming face to face with ourselves, we see ourselves in perspective, dependent upon those powers beyond us and interdependent with those around us.

When we acknowledge this basic condition of our existence, our common patterns of dividing and grouping people become irrelevant. For in the eyes of God we are all children. We each bring distinctive gifts to our lives together. But among us, before God, there are no hierarchies of status or class. There are no groups who receive preferential treatment. Greek and Jew, slave and free, male and female, adult and child—all of us engage each other as brothers and sisters. The stamp of God's image is impressed on each of our lives. Each of us is therefore sacred and of worth. No one is excluded. Anyone lost by human standards—through illness, birth into outcast classes, even through acts of crime—is the object of God's quest. Like the lost sheep, each is sought until found and returned to the fold, secure in the relationship with the shepherd and at one with the flock.

The growing awareness of our interdependence with the whole of humanity has a subsequent implication. Jacobi observes that *as the scope of our consciousness increases so does our capacity for judgments*.[17] This awareness does not make life easier. It carries with it the burden of responsibility to make decisions in the midst of the ambiguities of life. No longer able to rely on the *childish* patterns of dividing right or wrong by perpetuating customs, rules and laws accepted without question from the authority of parents, school, church, or government, we are confronted with the necessity of weighing the good in any situation against the evil that also exists in it. Such a task is not easy.[18] Consequently, it should not surprise us that, when we are confronted with this step in our pilgrimage through life, we will often shrink back into the comforts of a less demanding expression of consciousness. Such is the character of human behavior in all its finitude. A growing awareness of the demands of the wilderness frightened some of the early Hebrews to the point they would rather have returned to Egypt. The rich young man turned away from the one act that would have enabled him to enter into the intimacy of the relationship he sought with God. To give away his possessions, however, was too great a risk in the midst of his own insecurity. The corporate and personal flights of the disciples from their responsibilities as members of that fellowship may be traced to their unwillingness to accept the costs involved. Some may never recover from these moments of retreat and retrenchment. Still others, especially if nurtured by subsequent events, will, like Peter and most of the disciples, accept the responsibilities of their newly discovered understanding and continue their pilgrimages strengthened and renewed by the experience.

A third part of the task of discerning God's image in our lives involves *appropriating, as far as possible, the meanings of the events that we choose as the organizing centers for our perceiving, believing and doing.* If, with Christians down through the ages, we choose to order our lives around the events caught up in the life, death, and resurrection of Jesus Christ, we find ourselves imitating what we believe would be the attitude and responses he would make. But this task, as Jacobi pointed out, is not without its problems. It is all too easy to imitate some part of that event rather than to take up the whole range of its meanings. She observes that it has been a continuing temptation for some Christians to aspire to the imitation of the perfection of Jesus as the Son of God in the exercise of spiritual discipline and otherworldliness.[19] It has also been a temptation for other Christians to attempt to walk in his footsteps by living a highly ethical life of service and good works. Both approaches to the Christ event, however, ignore the full participation of Jesus in the ambiguities of human existence, and the fact that any real appropriation of that event would involve living in the crucible of both suffering and celebration.

All of us work on these four tasks throughout our lives. They are integral to our movement from the unreflective participation of children in the faith responses of the community to the conscious commitment adults may make to the meanings of the faith experience of the community. One of my contentions has been that childlikeness reveals something of the quality of a mature faith. This is not the only way to talk about faithfulness. But the image of childlikeness enables us to hold in tension the awareness of our own dependence upon God and the possibility of being conscious of who we are as we are known by God. It likewise yields important clues about what it means to be faithful. These clues may reveal how far we have progressed in our personal and corporate journeys of faith. They may illuminate the nature of our relationship to our Creator.

Clues for a Mature Faith in Childlikeness

Among the most confusing of the paradoxes of the Christian life is to be found in Jesus' words to the disciples that they could not receive the kingdom of heaven unless they became like children. Jesus' admonition is to be taken seriously, especially in the perspective of our discussion of maturing faith and emerging identity being related to the task of giving up childish ways of speaking, thinking, and acting.

Hans-Reudi Weber, in a provocative study of New Testament texts on the relationship of children to the kingdom of heaven, makes it clear that the words of Jesus are not to be taken literally. Rather, Jesus uses the child as a metaphor to reveal that the disciples' interest in being the greatest in the kingdom is misguided.[20] Weber observes that the relevant passages emphasize that the disciples must learn to think differently about their relationship to the Kingdom. They must turn and no longer look out for the greatest, but see "the little ones," or (as in Matthew's context) the children sitting in their midst, as exemplars of the qualities essential for receiving the kingdom of heaven. "In Jesus' teaching this expression always relates to the last judgment, and it is connected with stern exhortations and a call to a new way of life in the here and now."[21] It is this turning in perspective that is crucial if one is to receive the kingdom.

To receive the kingdom like a child, however, qualifies the nature of our relationship to the kingdom of God. The metaphorical use of the child clearly indicates that we are not to become children. To be childish is not appropriate. Instead, as Weber points out, the emphasis is on receiving the kingdom as a child might receive it. Especially within the context of the Markan and Lukan versions, the child functions as a metaphor for "objective humility." "Children are not necessarily more humble than adults," Weber reminds us, "but being dependent, they look for help from adults as a matter of course." They are "those who receive. As such, they become a metaphor of confident faith. To receive God's Kingdom like a child means to beg and claim this Kingdom like a child claims food and love. It means to receive with empty hands."[22]

Confident faith is integral to the identity of a person. Yet the confidence that supports most adults is not to be found in empty hands. Indeed, the greed, the self-centeredness, and the quest for security that dominate most of our lives would indicate that we commonly approach life with our hands as full as possible. We argue, consequently, over who is the greatest among us. We live, therefore, by baffling reflections. We, like the Corinthians, persist in childish behavior. Hence, those teachings of Jesus confront us just as they did the disciples with the nature of our relationship to all of creation. Is it to be found in the clenched fist or the open hand? As we explore what it means to receive the events and relationships of life with the open hands of a child, we may discover the fullness of the interdependence of faith and identity in the pilgrimage through life.

In the first place, one of the most obvious characteristics of children is their playfulness. It allows them to engage in life seriously without being overwhelmed and burdened by it. Indeed, it is through play that children most characteristically receive and organize the experience of life. Erikson has observed that the reciprocal character of human interaction "simply belongs to a growing organism's very existence in space and time . . . to *go at* things and people in a way that may invite playful mutuality. . . ."[23] Johann Huizinga, in his classic treatment of the function of play in culture, comes to a similar conclusion: "The great archetypal activities of human society are all permeated with play from the start." Whether we turn to language, myth, or rituals; or to religious, social, or political contexts; we discover that people have, from the first, "played" with the resources of their worlds.[24]

Huizinga traces four elements in play that may help us understand how it clarifies the admonition of Jesus. Play is, first of all, freedom. "Play is superfluous." It can be entered into at will. It "can be deferred or suspended at any time. It is never imposed by physical necessity or moral duty. It is never a task. It is done at leisure, during 'free time.' Only when play is a recognized cultural function—a rite, a ceremony—is it bound up with notions of obligation and duty."[25] Play involves engaging life with open hands—freely responding to the events and circumstances in which we may find ourselves. It may be seen in the actions of the infant exploring what can be done with a ball. It may also be seen whenever an adult engages a task as a challenge to be engaged rather than as a duty to be performed. Play feeds the imagination. It underscores a basic openness to the possibilities in life.

Huizinga describes a second characteristic of play as stepping out of "'real' life into a temporary sphere of activity with a disposition all of its own."[26] It involves the capacity to suspend one's involvement in the trials, tribulations, and tasks of everyday living in order to enter freely into the world of "make believe," the "world we would like to experience," "the world to come," the "kingdom of God." Such an attitude is crucial for those seeking to share in the communitas event described in the second chapter. Huizinga recognized the fine line between the seriousness of real life and the seriousness of play. It is a fine line that we readily recognize when we step back for a moment. When we tell children, youth or colleagues to quit "playing around and get down to business," the serious nature of play is clearly seen as second-rate. When we hear a magnificent violinist or watch a basketball game in which the sheer exertion of the players is beautiful to behold, however, our attention is riveted by the power of play that is serious. Such first-rate play transforms the drabness of our lives. Such seriousness obviously does not negate the seriousness of work, but it does put it in perspective. We discover, with Martha, that there is a time when it may be more important to sit at the feet of Jesus than to cook the meal that would feed him.

It is this capacity to play that frees the young to have visions and the elderly to dream. A dream or vision is never a reality, but it frees us to toil in the seriousness of work. The visions of the Promised Land, the other side of the Jordan, Gilead, or the sweet by-and-by that haunted the singing of the American slaves captured the spirit of play among those who were most seriously oppressed. They knew better than anyone else that they did not live in the Promised Land. But it did not prevent them from playing with the possibility. In their "pretending," they entered into the promise of that vision. Open-handed, they approached the kingdom.

A third characteristic of play is to be found in its limited nature. "It is 'played out' within certain limits of time and place."[27] Huizinga reminds us that when we play, our activity has both a beginning and an ending. But even when it is over, it continues to live on, both in our memories and in the traditions we create to "repeat" the event. Consequently, basketball, checkers, or tag may be repeated time and again. But we never play the game twice in the same way. Much of the fascination of play is in the changes that take place in the familiar. There is always an element of surprise and mystery in the expected. Is that not true of our relationship to God? We have the laws, the commandments, the teachings of Jesus; but in each new encounter we have the possibility of seeing into the "meanings of life" in a new way. We discover new courses of action and new possibilities for responding.

Play also imposes order upon space. There is usually a playing field of some kind to set the boundaries for our activities. It may be as limited as the checkerboard or as large as a football field. It may contain the boundaries imposed by the number and range of notes on the piano or by the variety of colors available to the artist at a given moment. It is in the midst of these limits of time and space that we play. They become, not limits to be held in our tight fists, but resources to be accepted gratefully. It is in the interaction with these limits that we discern the rhythm, harmony, and beauty of the created order around us.

A final characteristic of play, according to Huizinga, is the rules that govern all play. Rules are significant because "they determine what 'holds' in the temporary world circumscribed by play." They are binding and "allow no doubt."[28] Whenever someone breaks the rules, the game is over—at least until the transgressor agrees to accept the rules as understood by those involved. Huizinga observes that in play no one creates more disturbance than the "spoilsport," because this person refuses to accept the rules so that the game can proceed.

The traditions, creeds, doctrines, and institutional structures that accrue to the events we choose as the organizing centers for our lives function in our lives much like the rules in our games. The liturgy, for example, establishes a set of guidelines for the celebration or "play" of a congregation. It sets limits on what we do and say. We are led through certain words and actions. We do things as prescribed. And yet, within that same structure, worship from week to week is never quite the same. Just as the hymns, prayers, lessons, and sermon change, so do the attitudes and expectations of those involved. The circumstances surrounding the worship service vary. So the familiar becomes new for those familiar enough with the "rules" to see and hear the differences.

Not unlike the rules of a child's play, the structures of our lives are fragile. We spend much time defending them and propping them up. We impose them on people who view life differently or who have chosen to respond to other centers for identifying who they are and what they are about. And, like the rules of a game, they are easily broken. We can see this pattern in the way people "shop" for congregations that "play" by "rules" they can affirm. We can discern it in the resistance of some to engaging in activities others believe are crucial. Consequently, we find some people who write letters to their legislators about the injustices of the world, and we find others calling for the personal conversion of the unjust to effect a moral transformation of society. Each group believes it is playing by the "correct" rules. When groups disagree, the resulting squabble over whose rules to use often sounds much like that heard during a sandlot ball game among children. We usually see these conflicts as harmful. Actually, they illustrate the importance of rules in guiding our interactions at all levels of life. The conflict has to do not with the necessity of rules, but with their relative value.

Play begins with the premise that through finite structure we may perceive sublime beauty and truth. As such, then, play is central to the experience of the holy. It underlies the reason why many people describe the experience of the indwelling presence of the Holy Spirit as a "happening" or a "celebration." These are common terms for joyous time-and-space-bound events. They are often used similarly to describe a party that embodies the very dynamics of playing. They are increasingly used to point to a basic part of the experience of corporate worship.

To view the kingdom as a child means we would recognize the limited character of the "rules" we follow. Jesus made this point when he challenged the allegiance of the Jews to the Law. "Do not suppose that I have come to abolish the law," but rather "to complete" it (Matt. 5:17, NEB). The laws, doctrines, creeds, and disciplines of the church are historically significant, but they are all limited. Our Methodist, Presbyterian, Baptist, Catholic, pentecostal, evangelical, orthodox, and liberal variations both reveal and inhibit the power of the event that serves as the source of our mutual and distinct existence. Each of these structured expressions of that event has normative and revelatory power for the lives of people. The history of the church witnesses to that fact. There are saints in many traditions. But to cling to any tradition as the normative tradition for all people is to perpetuate the debate among the disciples regarding who is the greatest. Humble obedience calls us to recognize that we impose limited structures and finite expressions on eternal truths.

And yet, these structures of institution, belief, and worship that give shape to our corporate lives and personal pilgrimages are crucial. One cannot play a game "in general." It is only in the specificity of limited structures that we finite creatures enter into and receive the blessings and joy of the infinite kingdom. Like children, we receive the kingdom in the interplay of the real and the envisioned. We live in the awareness that the structures gathered around the events that inform our lives function normatively. At the same time they are clues to the experience of those whose lives are informed by other events. To acknowledge this paradox is to recognize that we live in the tension of rational and irrational forces. It is to affirm the fact that we encounter both the conscious and the unconscious dimensions of our lives in all that we do. It is to accept both the limits of human existence and the stamp of God's impression, which penetrates those same limits with the possibilities of infinity. In play, with its links to the paradoxical nature of the human experience, we may discern one clue for the life of faith.

A second clue may be found in the way a childlike person's vulnerability empowers others. The child enters the world without any defenses. The child leaves the warmth and security of the mother's womb to live in an environment dominated by the will and whims of others. The child is completely at our disposal. Without any say in the matter, the child is fully vulnerable, risking all by trusting in those of us who have been given the responsibility of caring for him or her.

The vulnerability of the child is exemplified by the servant role Jesus assumed. Jesus dramatized the nature of this relationship when he washed the feet of the disciples. In that act, as Walter Brueggeman reminds us, he knelt before them, placed himself at their disposal, came to them without defense. He risked everything.[29] Similarly, children come to us, simply being in the service of those around them. "Get the paper." "Give me a hug." "Be a big girl and run next door for Mother." It is in serving others that we experience, not only the vulnerability characteristic of childhood, but the lifestyle of those who choose to be disciples of Jesus the Christ. For it is vulnerability that is stamped into the character and approach of those who call him Master.

A significant thing happens when a person chooses to be a servant to others. That posture "bestows on the other mastery."[30] Such an action means we take other people seriously. Children confer upon parents, teachers, grandparents, and pastors a mastery that sometimes confuses us. We hear it whenever a child claims that his or her father can beat up the parent of a friend. We encounter it in their requests to do impossible tasks—which they believe we can do. We see it in the child who insists upon clinging to an abusive parent. We are confronted by it through the child who may ask if we are God or Jesus.

The consequences of these experiences are dependent upon the sensitivity and character of those who function as "masters." As often happens to servants, their experience may degrade rather than enhance. All too often, as with Jesus, it leads to crucifixion—the death of self in the service of another. The experience of the cross is common to children. They participate daily in events that confront them with the life-giving and life-destroying power we as parents, teachers, and ministers have over their lives. They die to our dreams for their lives. They die to our plans for the day. They die to our expectations of how they shall dress, talk, or act. They die to our lack of acceptance of their gifts. They die in the structures we set up to control them for their own so-called education and growth. They die to our own confusions, doubts, and harried schedules. They die to our indulgence of them. Vulnerability even to the daily processes of dying for others is a common experience of children and a basic characteristic of the follower of Jesus Christ.

A third clue in childlikeness for our pilgrimages of faith may be found in children's expectations that they are growing. Such people are filled both with "incredible expectation and rigorous discipline."[31] We do not have to search hard for illustrations. The child's expectation of growing permeates almost every activity in which he or she is engaged. We can see it in the struggle of young children learning to walk. They approach the task with great anticipation. Indeed, they expect to walk. The only question is when they will sense they are ready to make those first unaided steps. In the meantime, they practice walking all over the house holding on to every object available to them.

Again, such expectation is not confined to children; it is simply most completely caught up in their experience. It is evident in the concert pianist who hears the outpouring of melody and harmonies in a sheet of music. It is evident in the farmer who perceives a highly productive orchard in an eroded and worn-out field. Such people are obedient to the order inherent in the harmony of creation. The glory of what is possible—whether it be walking, talking, learning the multiplication tables, performing a difficult sonata, or rebuilding an old automobile engine—dominates their attention. These are the dreams and the visions described by the prophet. They belong not only to the young in years, but to the young in spirit of any age. They are the source of the capacity to plunge into each day with the expectation that today is not only the day that the Lord has made, but that in this day the glory of the Lord shall be revealed. For such people, the future is as real and lively as the present.

But growth is not only dependent upon our eager

anticipation of the future. It is nurtured with rigorous discipline. The distinction may be seen in the life of Peter. His expectations for the life and work of the followers of Jesus were indeed high. But his anticipation did not involve the discipline characteristic of his life after the events of Holy Week. The transformation in Peter that occurred in his encounter with the resurrected Christ had to do, not so much with his commitment to the dream they shared for a community of love and peace and justice, but with the intensity and perseverance with which he pursued that dream. The dream no longer belonged simply to Jesus. It had now become Peter's very reason for existence.

The discipline that nurtures the growth in a childlike person does not consist of subordinating or controlling the will of another until it conforms with external expectations. Nor is it to be confused with restriction. Instead, Patrick Swazos Hinds hints at its true character when he describes "discipline" as "dedication." It is an internal process integrating the energies, skills, commitments, values, and dreams of a person and channeling them in an intentionally chosen activity. Such discipline is essential, says Hinds, because without it, a person loses respect for her or his own efforts.[32]

The intense discipline characteristic of the childlike person liberates rather than confines. It opens up possibilities rather than closes them off. Such people are the "innocents" of any age, because they are unfettered by the chains of the limits we impose upon ourselves and our actions. With God, they proclaim that anything is possible. We may call them naïve. But theirs is the faith that has brought new life and hope to the depressed and downtrodden throughout history.

A fourth clue manifests itself in the readiness of childlike people to trust so completely that they can willingly leave the security of familiar relationships, institutional roles, positions of status and power for the "wilderness" that lies beyond the known. This theme is deeply rooted in our religious heritage. Abraham and Sarah gathered up their family's belongings and ventured into the desert for a land "promised" to them. In doing so, they left the safety and security of family and friends, and the ordered stability of city life behind them. Perhaps the story of Noah is popular among children because he accepted the ludicrous assignment to engage in a venture into the uncharted and unknown future. The paradigm of such stories, of course, is the exodus of the Hebrews from Egypt under the leadership of Moses, Aaron, and Miriam. Without the weaponry to defend themselves against their Egyptian masters, without any indication of a steady source of daily food, and without a clear sense of direction, they entered the unknown wilderness of the Sinai.

The wilderness is not alien to our own experience—nor is it unfamiliar to the child. The first time children are left in the church nursery, they encounter the wilderness. For many children, school is a wilderness. In spite of all the preparation parents may make, children's anxiety over what the big kids will do; where the classrooms, lunchroom, and restrooms are; and whether or not they will be accepted; only reveals that this new "adventure," as we adults call it, is as alien and forbidding as the most barren wilderness. It continues to be a wilderness for many—confusing, frightening, overwhelming them for years.

The wilderness is familiar to most of us because there are times when we have been thrust into it—often against our will. Through the loss of a job, an unexpected or unwanted divorce, the death of a loved one, a congregational or community controversy, we find ourselves in the midst of a strange and desolate land. Often, like some of the Hebrews, we want to head safely back into the familiarity and security of previous patterns and structures—even when they have been prisons or slave camps of the spirit. In the course of wandering through these wastelands of our lives, we may eventually discover the sustaining elements in the desert. We may stumble into the qualities of trusting obedience in the midst of the confusion that engulfs us.

The childlike trust in the experience in the wilderness, however, is one that is usually chosen. If, with Abraham, we can trust so intensely the call to leave for the promised land, or if, with Moses, we can accept so completely God's guidance that we are able to leave the comforts of home and risk the ridicule of our own people to effect their liberation from the bondage of slavery, we will approach each day with the childlikeness Jesus described.

The willingness to enter the wilderness is crucial for our lives as the people of God, because it is in the barren desert that we discover most clearly the faithfulness of God. When the Hebrews thought they were lost, they received the gifts of the pillars of fire and smoke to guide them. When they thought they would die of starvation, they received the gift of manna. When they believed they would die of thirst, they were led to a spring of fresh water. When they lost a sense of order and purpose, they received the gift of God's covenantal love—each with open hands.

When we believe we are alone, we discover the power of relationships uncluttered by social pretenses. When our resources are gone, we are open to receive the gifts of basic sustenance and strength with gratitude—even if they are not in the latest style, or replete with the additives, extra sugar or enriched colors we have come to expect. When the dreams others have for us or our own fantasies will no longer work, we may be able to hear the voice of God calling us. Such people may be found among the blind who can see, among the crippled who can leap with joy, among those who never felt they had anything to say but who can nevertheless speak with wisdom and insight, and among the elderly who still dream dreams and have visions. Their trust in the unknown is such that they can venture into the wilderness—frightened perhaps, but deliberately—steadfast in the faith that God is with them.

A fifth clue for our faith pilgrimages may be found in the security childlike people have in their own existence. Their sense of identity is firmly grounded in the relationships that nurture and sustain them. Comfortable with their dependence upon God as creator and redeemer, upon parents, friends, neighbors, colleagues, and children as the source of daily strength and well-being, they confront the events of each day.

They are not dependent upon the temporal structures and

rituals of a society to tell them "who they are." They live through the ambiguity and confusion that surrounds them with a clarity of purpose and an outpouring of energy that often surprise us. They lack the self-consciousness that often inhibits us. They convey a spontaneity that is disarming.

Again the paradigm for this characteristic of childlikeness is to be found in children. We can see it in the wholehearted responses they make to the events and circumstances of their lives. When babies are hungry, they tend to be hungry "all over." When they are uncomfortable, their whole being is uncomfortable. When they are happy, their eyes light up, their fingers are busy, their toes wiggle, and they squirm with a total sense of pleasure. Such responses are characteristic of the childlike teenager or adult as well. Their excitement, joy, sorrow, and pain are experiences that permeate the whole of their being. It is "infectious," touching the lives of others out of the center of their own responses to the events of living in a particular place at a given time in history.

This security in our own existence is what Paul describes as the "new life" in Christ. This gift, evident in the responses of the young child, is the promise held out to all. Secure in that relationship in Christ, we are unencumbered by the chains of family and society that constrain and inhibit us. Consequently we can respond to each day praising God with the psalmist—for the glory of God is at hand. We can sing and dance with joy. We can live in peace—even in the crossfire of the tensions of daily life. For in that gift we live in the harmony of God's creation. Such security in the midst of all the evils and pain recorded on the daily news and encountered in our own lives is characteristic of the childlikeness of the faithful person.

Summary

To be childlike, in other words, requires continuing growth. It involves the constant reminder that, before God, we are all children. The differences in maturity between the youngest child and the oldest adult are very small when contrasted with the differences between the faithfulness of any human being and the faithfulness of God. So, in the incorporation of the deepest meanings of the experience of children into our faith lives as adults, we acknowledge and affirm the authority of God more fully in our own lives.

This process engages us in a pilgrimage through life. At every turn and in each situation, we are confronted with certain tasks to move us from the faith responses that are undifferentiated from those of the community that nurtures us to a conscious commitment to the meanings that have sustained the community. These tasks involve clarifying our relationship to the place in which we find ourselves and to the significant events around which the community is formed. They also include recognizing and affirming the presence of possibilities—both negative and positive—which we have heretofore hidden from ourselves, and the imprint of God in both our personal and corporate lives.

That journey does not change our relationship to God. We remain as children, united in a common dependence upon the mercy of our Creator. Yet, through that journey, that relationship may be altered. We may choose to respond by affirming the limits of creation as the resources for creative playing. We may celebrate, in the midst of our vulnerability, our dependence upon God. We may anticipate the possibilities of each turn in our journeys through life, expecting that with each challenge and task we will extend our understanding and skills. We may enter the wilderness of the unknown that lies before us, trusting in the continuing presence of God. In the process we witness to the freedom to live in the structures of this world but unencumbered by them. We live open-handed, claiming our dependence upon God.

CHAPTER 4

TEACHING
A Responsibility of the Community of Faith

"Within our community God has appointed, in the first place apostles, in the second place prophets, thirdly teachers . . . ." (I Cor. 12:28a, NEB)

In our society we tend to limit our understanding of the experiences of childhood to people under a given age. The twelfth year is often seen as the dividing line between childhood and adolescence—its sequel in our view of the life cycle. At the same time, there are moments when we look upon childhood as an experiential condition. In this sense, the status of being children has nothing to do with age. It has to do with the relationship people have to the expectations others have of them or to the limits of their experience in a given situation. If they respond with naïveté, ignorance, innocence, or a sense of powerlessness, we often call them "mere children" or "babes in the wood." In our assessment of the depth and breadth of their words and actions, we may say they lack experience. They may be unaware of the complexities of life. They may lack information or knowledge requisite for making difficult decisions. They may lack the historical and cultural perspective to foresee the potential consequences of their actions. They may be unable to respond with sensitivity to the nuances of the community's heritage or identity. They may lack the skills to act decisively and effectively. This happens when people of any age sense that they are outsiders, strangers, neophytes, or greenhorns. It happens when personal experience and community expectations do not coincide. Such people stand at some threshold in the life of the community and participate in it as learners. We call them novitiates, apprentices, or students.

These threshold experiences, however, are not static. Through formal and informal procedures, people become familiar with the resources and expectations of the community and begin to use them with greater confidence. They may gradually perceive the interdependence of contemporary experience and prior events. They may develop the sensitivity to respond creatively to the varieties of expectations of those around them. They may be able to risk personal status and recognition to preserve, to extend, or to alter the values and commitments of the community for yet another circumstance or situation. We may find ourselves turning to them for guidance or direction, or to accomplish some task. We may call them wise or wonderful, sensitive or counselor, leader or mature. Such people no longer participate in the community on its periphery. They are seen by others, and view themselves, as living at its center.

A paradox of human life occurs in this rhythmic interplay between our recurring experiences of new and old, strange and familiar, impotence and power, ignorance and knowledge, or naïveté and wisdom. In the first instance, when we encounter the new or strange, we participate in an event with the dependence characteristic of children. We appear to be strangers and out of place. What we know seems irrelevant. What we can do seems inappropriate. We feel childish. Growing familiarity increases our security. We develop new skills. We see connections between what we already know and what we are experiencing. We begin to feel "at home." We begin to have a sense of being "mature" or "grown-up" (as a young child might say). Then a new situation confronts us with the sensation of being children again—requiring new perspectives and skills.

In the previous chapter, I argued that in the Christian community the very qualities of childhood we try to outgrow are among the major goals of mature persons. But there is a difference between the unconscious experience characteristic of children in this process and its conscious experience in maturity. The writer of the Gospel According to St. Matthew alludes to this paradoxical interplay when he claims we should be innocent as doves *and* wise as serpents (Matt. 10:16, RSV). The difference has to do with how conscious we are of our situation. In being childlike, we do not lose our innocence. Childlikeness is shown in the integrity we reveal in our decisions and actions. The simplicity of our thought may be evident in our singlemindedness and not in any lack of awareness of the complexity of life's issues. Our vulnerability is not our weakness but our strength. Our expectations involve growth and the extension of our knowledge and experience, and not the ability to control and direct. Our trust is located in those things unseen rather than seen. Our security is in knowing ourselves as the children of God and not in our status or position in life.

The recurring lifelong pattern of entering and moving through the life and expectations of the community is not an accidental one. It does not take place in haphazard fashion if the community has any sense of loyalty to its past or any sense of destiny in the future. In this chapter, we shift our attention to teaching as one of the functions of a community concerned with introducing those on its threshold into its life and empowering them to contribute to its future.

Teaching is not the only activity of a community concerned with these two tasks, but it is one of the most important. Teaching always occurs within a community, and if it is effective, always for the sake of the community. Its importance is acknowledged by a people who:

1. recall, rehearse, and interpret their histories for new circumstances and situations;

2. live toward a future that not only intrudes on the present but also calls them into a destiny to be fulfilled;

3. take seriously the interdependence of the generations as the meeting ground of past-remembered and future-envisioned;

4. view individual and group events in the pilgrimage of faith as the occasions for renewing corporate identity and purpose;

5. remember that it is in their commitment to the content of the faith of the community that the identity of its members is revealed.

When a community emphasizes the importance of teaching, it assumes responsibility for exploring and opening up meanings deeply rooted in the hidden recesses of the human experience. It orders and makes sense out of the relationships that structure the lives of its members. It connects those unexpected experiences of communitas with the meanings and relationships in the corporate heritage.

The Nature of Teaching

Both our image of, and our approach to, the task of teaching have changed significantly during the past several years. I sense the changes in the conversations of parents and long-time teachers, as well as among my colleagues; who often wonder whatever happened to the teacher who knew what had to be taught, whose authority was not questioned, and whose role was clearly affirmed in the life of the congregation and community. I see the changes in the new caricatures the media are creating to replace the Ichabod Cranes, Mr. Chipses, Mary Poppinses, and the "old maid" teachers of bygone days. Now we find teachers depicted as conflict managers and human relations experts, through the likes of Gabe Kotter and the "White Shadow," whose compassionate toughness regularly and successfully penetrates the resistance of the most difficult students. I observe the changes whenever I see a teacher sitting with students in a circle, rather than at a desk before them. Perhaps these changes are most evident in current descriptions of the teachers' role. They are called leaders, enablers, and facilitators, rather than instructors and scholars. Such changes are not accidental. They involve a radical shift in the nature and function of teaching in our educational institutions.

This shift has been helpful at several points. It has heightened the sensitivity of teachers to students' diverse capacities and cultural backgrounds, increased their responsiveness to students' interests, and encouraged them to be more creative in constructing learning environments. It has reminded educators that people take the initiative for much of their own learning and contribute to the instruction of their peers. It has made possible the recognition that people learn in diverse ways and therefore need a variety of teaching-learning environments. And it has, to mention its most significant consequence, reminded teachers that their efforts must be both human and humane.

But not all the effects of this shift have been positive. In fact, it has precipitated several unfortunate consequences for those who view education as a social and historical function. It has triggered a loss of historical perspective and a corresponding lack of vision for the future on the part of both teachers and learners. It has lulled us into naïvely assuming that learning inevitably takes place once we have created appropriate conditions for motivating people. It has contributed to our tendency to confine teaching to schools. It has tended to reduce the corporate character of the educational process to a privatistic interaction between teacher and learner. It has perpetrated a relentless search for "never-fail" strategies and procedures and has almost totally ignored the ancient quest for truth dominating earlier views of education. In the church, moreover, it has diverted teachers' attention from their distinctive function in the life of the community of faith, often making them representatives of the status quo, rather than agents of God's continuing creativity. And, perhaps most significantly, it has made teaching subservient to learning in the educational enterprise in both church and school. In consequence, researchers and teachers tend to focus on how people learn rather than on handing down and reformulating cherished values and practices to people in new circumstances.

These problems are serious. They account for much of the malaise in our public schools and much of the apathy in our church schools. They reinforce the role confusion of teachers and inhibit others in our society who teach in a wide variety of other settings from grasping the significance of their efforts. They perpetuate the ahistorical character of much contemporary education. They all too often deny students the resources of the past that might help them understand their present experience. They blind us to the necessary interdependence of teaching and learning. And they perpetuate the deeply rooted view in our society that teaching is something that happens in schools and nowhere else in the community.

Teaching, as an activity of the community, involves more than these old and new images convey. Perhaps my point can be seen in a description of several characteristics drawn from a view of teaching as a link between the resources of the community's past and the potential in its future.

Teaching is a historical activity. Its sources and purposes are rooted in the heritage of the community. It transmits values, attitudes, and ideas from the past into the present, in the hope that they will influence people's decisions regarding their corporate future. It hands on skills refined in the past, with the expectation that they will prove useful in coping with contemporary problems and tasks and in exploring the frontiers of the unknown. Teaching specifically inducts a new generation into the life of the community, anticipating that the corporate identity of the people will thereby be extended into the future.

Teaching is a corporate activity. It always occurs within the community for the sake of the community. Maxine Greene has observed that the "identity and meaning" of a culture or community depend upon the extent to which children or those immigrants or converts who stand on its threshold "internalize characteristic attitudes, beliefs, skills, and values."[1] Jesus' teaching, for example, was shaped by historic Judaism. Even though his words often sounded new to his hearers, Jesus' teaching was grounded in the ancient laws, customs, and perspectives of the children of Abraham and Sarah. The teaching of the disciples was nurtured both by that same context and by the unique fellowship of that motley band of Jesus' followers who lived, ate, slept, argued, prayed, and served together. Through their conversations, Jesus sought to convey specific attitudes, beliefs, skills, and values that were deeply rooted in their common heritage, but had the potential to make a distinctive contribution the future of all people. The fellowship of the disciples—its roots in their Hebraic past and its future in the church, the body of Christ—similarly forms the corporate and historic context for our own teaching. Our teaching, consequently, is always judged by its faithfulness to the central commitments and values of the community, through which we understand and express our corporate identity. It can never be confined to the limits of our own individual experience.

Teaching is an urgent activity. Any community is only one generation from extinction. That is why the children of a community are so important for the continuity of its life and structures. That is also why teaching is so important for the continuity of its identity. Without teachers, the past is closed to the young and the newcomer. Its events lose the power to inform people's decisions and commitments for the future. Its meanings become lifeless. Its institutions and traditions become relics; intriguing perhaps, but essentially useless.

If we accept Robert McAfee Brown's view of faith as involving the appropriation of meanings deeply rooted in our common heritage, then the depth of our commitments is dependent on the availability of the resources of the past. It makes little sense for us to call ourselves Christians, for instance, if the events surrounding the life, death, and resurrection of Jesus Christ are left unexplored and unexamined. Teaching is the primary approach taken by a community to open up the meanings of past events, to confront the circumstances of the present from the perspective of those meanings, and to explore the implications of decisions about the course of our future. The focus of teaching is not on the past. It makes use of the past to shape the future.

Teaching is an eschatological activity. The community's sense of destiny draws upon imagery and meanings located in its originating events. The rehearsal of that past event provides the impetus to move into the future. Teachers recall the stories surrounding that originating event. They alert those they teach to their corporate and personal destiny by recalling and interpreting that event. They provide resources and experiences to prepare people to embody that event. Just as parochial and public school teachers may perceive the continuity of the values and ideals of the nation in the children they teach, so Sunday school or Confraternity of Christian Doctrine teachers may envision the next generation of cross-bearers in the members of their classes.

Teaching is a relational activity. It involves a two-way relationship for the teacher. On the one hand, the teacher is responsible to the community whose values and commitments are the subject of the teacher's task. On the other hand, the teacher is responsive to the people entering the life of that community. In the former relationship, the teacher "always represents the public world," Greene has written, "with its institutions, its predefined forms, its categories and disciplines." Whenever teachers engage people as students, they speak "to them in a continuum that differs from and often collides with the one" in which they as students exist.[2] Teachers go about their task as participants in a community, mediators of a tradition, and agents of a shared vision. In this relationship, teachers are expected to be faithful to the heritage of the community.

In the latter relationship, teachers are also responsive to those being introduced to the customs and practices of the community (for the sake of both students and community). Hence, teachers approach their tasks sensitive to the diversity of students' interests, capacities, and needs, as well as the influence of their specific cultural heritages, and the distinctive character of people's learning styles.

Books on teaching unfortunately tend to envision the teacher as functioning in only one of these two relations. The resulting debate often centers over the primacy of content (relation to the community) or process (relation to learners). The split is evident in the tension many educators pose between subject matter and experience, or between the authority of the instructor and the responsibility of the student. Teaching, however, has to do with both sides of the debate. Whenever the interdependence of past, present, and future is taken seriously, teaching encompasses content and process, past and present, responsibility and sensitivity.

Teaching is an intentional activity of the community. It embodies "purposeful action," Maxine Greene has observed. It does not take place through whim, some consensus over topic of common interest, or by the formative influence of the hidden curricula embedded in the structures, patterns of relating, customs, and assumed values of an institution or society. Instead, the intentional character of teaching may be discerned when certain people either assume responsibility for introducing, or are designated to introduce, others into the community's corporate past, share with them its common vision, and engage them in the interaction of the two in the specific demands of the present moment.

The ongoing life of the community is an important educational force in the lives of all its members. Any activity or concern in the life of the community may be appropriated through the processes of enculturation, as anthropologists and sociologists have demonstrated so well. Such processes, however, are for the most part unconscious. Teaching is one activity of the community that lifts those values and practices into consciousness and becomes the occasion for the deliberate transmission and interpretation of those parts of its life deemed to be of greatest value. Teaching always occurs within the context of these ongoing patterns of enculturation. Those who teach, however, "intend" people to view that context in certain ways. They expect their students to "perform in particular ways, to do particular tasks, to impose increasingly complex orders upon their worlds."[3] Hence, teaching is not a passive activity. It intrudes (when effective) deliberately and sensitively into the growth processes of people. This assertive activity is undertaken with the aim that the values, attitudes, and behaviors deemed important by the community will be appropriated, internalized, and used by their students. Teachers, in other words, engage in what Urban Holmes has called the "imposition of meaning," deeply rooted in the life of the community, upon those who seek to understand it or participate in it.[4]

Some teachers are designated, especially in schools. But many who teach do not assume this clearly specific role. They teach, however, whenever they assume responsibility to open up to another person certain basic meanings or practices of the community. This latter approach to teaching is not always organized or structured. Its intermittent patterns are so common we often do not recognize their true value or purpose. A bystander observes a child about to run into the street and intervenes to warn the child of the possible consequences and to affirm certain behaviors crucial to personal and public safety. A clerk in the grocery store stops a shopper to describe how one can tell if a pineapple is ripe or not. A newscaster adds a commentary to the report of an event, identifying its relationship to a certain value system. A parent guides the child's first efforts to mow the lawn so that the finished job will measure up to neighborhood standards. A child shows a friend the way to play hop-scotch. A long-time member of a congregation instructs a visitor sitting nearby on the way worship is conducted in that place. These illustrations are common, everyday occurrences. But they reveal at least two people in a social interaction. One intentionally intervenes in the life of the other to introduce him or her into practices, attitudes, or understandings integral to the corporate life in which both are found for the moment.

Teaching as an intentional action occurs whenever and wherever a people lives with a self-conscious identity as a community within the total human family. This corporate identity includes certain rituals, traditions, beliefs, attitudes, and behaviors considered crucial to expressing that identity.

Certain past events are considered formative for their corporate lives and often provide the scenario for their current self-understanding. Newcomers, whether by birth or immigration, will live as strangers or aliens in that community until they have entered into those meanings and processes to the point that they assume their presence. That process occurs, in part, in the community's deliberate efforts to transmit that experience from one generation to the next.

Teaching as an intentional action occurs, moreover, whenever and wherever a people is committed to introducing its young and newcomers into mysteries and meanings inherited from the past. Teaching assumes the passage of time. It has a historical perspective. In his description of the relation of faith to the past, Brown observes that the wealth of a community's heritage is never expended. The same phenomenon is observable in the teacher's use of the past. Indeed, the vitality and relevance of a community's past becomes evident only in the continued reworking of familiar material received from the past in the light of the always-changing contemporary issues and tasks influencing our perceptions and actions. When a community ceases to celebrate and explore its own past, it loses its urgency to teach.

Correspondingly, teaching is done whenever and wherever a people believes that the formative events from its past have the power to influence an unknown and incomprehensible future. Within the Christian community, we continue to assess the value of life by comparing our experiences to those of the ancient Hebrews in covenant with God. Our hope for the future is significantly influenced by our glimpse of the potential in human relationships revealed in the encounters Jesus had with the disciples and with those he met from day to day. We hold that the meanings of these ancient events are relevant for contemporary life. We assume they have value for the future. In our commitment to the potential value of the known for the unknown and the past for the future, we take seriously our efforts to introduce successive generations to the people, events, ideas, places, and circumstances that make up their heritage.

In static societies, characterized by Margaret Mead as perceiving little or no difference between the meaning of events in the past and those in contemporary life, the teaching of the community may well make for distinctions between the past received and the future envisioned. I contend, however, that even in the most protected of communities, the bombardment of external natural, social, and political forces continually requires them—through their teachers and other interpreters—to make new sense out of their past in light of the disruptions in their present situation.

Whether or not communities decide to keep the changes self-consciously before them may well depend upon their awareness of the flow of time itself. Some lose track of the distances between an original event and its sequels. Many in the church today perpetuate such a perspective in their attempts to use the Bible as a direct commentary on contemporary events, ignoring in the process almost two thousand years of history between the original and the contemporary event. The Israelites, with their keen sense of history, usually avoided this same trap. The Exodus, the formation of the kingdom under David, the eventual shattering and loss of that same kingdom, the exile into Babylon, and the return of the captives to Jerusalem were major events, each calling for an "updating" of an earlier national and spiritual self-understanding. The books of Ezra and Nehemiah, for example, illustrate this phenomenon in Israelite history. They describe the "new form" of Israel following "the dissolution of the old tribal confederation" with the exile into Babylon. This form, recognized by the prevailing government, took shape as a "community subject to the special law of God." "Submission to this law became the decisive token of membership of Israel and the Jerusalem religious community. The organic unity of the Old Israel was replaced by the circle of those who acknowledged the law. . . ." In principle, this change meant that the identity of the people, no longer restricted by geographical boundaries or family ties, now centered on the law and the temple. It effectively narrowed "the circle" so as to exclude some of the "old community," as well as expanded it to encompass non-Israelites who pledged allegiance to the law.[5] Teachers contribute significantly to such a task when they introduce the young and the newcomers of the community to their heritage. Through their teaching, they seek, not to extend the past blindly into the future, but to open it up for investigation and incorporation, to the end that it may be recreated for the situation and circumstances in which the current generation must live.

Who May Teach

I have insisted that the ministry of teaching belongs to the whole community. The community is ultimately responsible for introducing people into its life. The processes of introduction, however, are too fragile and too urgent to be left to chance, or even to the often-unconscious patterns of socialization to be found in any group. It is at this point that I believe John Westerhoff has gone too far in his critique of the American Christian commitment to the school as a primary vehicle for the church's teaching ministry. He (accurately, from my point of view) identifies numerous weaknesses in what he calls the "schooling-instructional paradigm;" the tendency to ignore the contribution of the learner to the community, to confuse teaching about religion with the nurture of faith, to institutionalize certain social and moral values that are contrary to those most closely identified with the historic Christian community. Westerhoff, however, tends to equate teaching with the institutions of the public and church schools. He ignores, in the process, the richness of the variety of designated teaching roles that exist in structures and institutions other than the schools, including the patterns of teaching made popular through the literary societies of the Chautauqua movement at the turn of the century and its successors in many of the nonacademic adult education movements in our own day; the instructional modes of "Each One Teach One" that Frank Laubach introduced to combat illiteracy, not only in many nations around the world, but also in our own; the problem-solving approaches of Paolo Freire and others who have encouraged oppressed people to develop their own powers to "perceive critically the way they exist in the world with which and in which they find themselves";[6] the consultative approaches of Peace Corps members, who participate in the life of the communities they served; the experts who have influenced the thinking of governmental, business, and other research organizations as outside observors; or the subliminal patterns developed by television personnel to influence the decisions of their viewers. Consequently, even as Westerhoff emphasizes in a helpful way the creative function of the unconscious patterns of socialization, as well as traditions, rituals, rites of passage, and other elements in the life of communities for inducting the young into their corporate lives, he displaces the cutting edge of the teaching role in the community. He loses sight of the historical character of the teaching task. And he undermines the distinctive but interdependent functions of teaching and learning. Even though every community may have its designated teachers, the teaching role in the community is not filled only by those who have been officially recruited, formally trained, and publicly certified. And yet, communities recruit, train, and certify teachers to ensure the transmission of the tradition and to prepare people to contribute to their corporate destiny. Their importance cannot be underestimated. Through their work, communities intentionally choose to extend their life through still another generation.

Everyone teaches at some time or another, but only a few are recognized as teachers by any community. Only a few, in spite of all the people whom schools and churches recruit and certify, are celebrated as people who "teach." Paul recognized the paradox I am describing. Teaching is a gift. Jesus had received that gift. He was called Rabbi—teacher—by those who sought him out to gaze upon him, as did Zaccheus, or to listen to him along with the crowds. Yet the role of teacher is also an earned one. In the final analysis, only those who have been taught can point to someone and declare him or her to be a teacher. A teacher is thereby one who is prepared with both the resources of the community and the capacity to respond to the questions and curiosity of students. Certification does not guarantee teaching. Neither does having a teaching job. Only a person's learning ultimately reflects that one has indeed taught.

The teaching in the community that creatively opens up the past and sensitively introduces people into the future takes place in and through people who embody specific qualities and characteristics. It is transmitted through those whose participation in, and identification with, the community is the source of their own identity. For Christians, that identity is grounded in the body of Christ as the framework for their corporate lives. The formative event of the community thus becomes the wellspring of a person's teaching. It is the content of teaching. It is the end of teaching. When we teach, we are credible to the extent that we identify with the historic meanings of that event as they are lived out in the historic community that gives our own lives direction and purpose.

Teaching is done by those whose sense of the future is inspired by the community's vision of its own sense of its destiny. Those who have no vision can "intend" nothing. They, in fact, condemn their students to live in a past that is perhaps known only in a limited manner. Such "teaching" is lifeless. It lacks purpose and ultimately any meaning to empower people to make decisions to give direction to their daily living, especially in the rapidly changing world we live in.

Effective teachers accept responsibility for the intentional shaping of the historic experience of the community. Teaching, Greene observes, is done "deliberately in situations never twice the same."[7] Therefore, responsible teaching cannot simply repeat received knowledge. It has to be recast for the always-new situation in which we find ourselves. This "deliberate" reformulation of the past for those seeking to participate with meaning and power in the present is the teacher's distinctive contribution to the community.

Teaching is done by those who courageously presume to choose from the vast wealth of resources received from the past and, just as daringly, choose to confront those they teach with their discoveries and conclusions. Teaching is, by nature, a disturbing activity. It tests and questions people. It elicits responses from them that alter perceptions, change courses of action, and require hard decisions. Teachers confront people with their finitude. They point to their bondage. They identify the sources of their security, and they question their idolatries. These actions require risk, challenge, and courage of the teachers.

The teaching of the community is done most effectively through those whose sensitivity to the capacities, needs, and situations of those they teach informs their decisions about what and how to teach. It is, of course, helpful for teachers to have the theoretical insights from learning, human development, and personality theories. It is more important, however, for teachers to be able to discern the growing edges of people at the point of their encounter with the resources and practices of the community.

What Teachers Do

As representatives of the community past and agents of the community future, the teachers' role is distinctively shaped by the mediating role they fill between the two. In their stance between community and student, that role is expressed in at least three ways.

In the first place, in the community of faith, *teachers incarnate meanings from the past for those they teach in the present.* The view of teaching I am suggesting here involves the vitality of a faith commitment. We cannot live in a vacuum. We are always confronted with the necessity of choosing among alternative ways of viewing and relating to significant past events.[8] Whatever our choice, its significance supersedes the power of other events. It illuminates and gives credence to what we do and say. We believe it is useful. It provides clues to guide our decisions and actions. It provides a reference point to assess the adequacy of what we believe and do. It becomes, as Brown suggests, normative for our lives.[9] With the intensification of our identification with those events, their content increasingly defines who we are.

That definition gives form and shape to our commitments. It gives direction to our lives. It infuses our existence with a sense of destiny. Our lives are not diffuse. They become focused. We have a contribution to make. The power of these incarnated limits is seen in the title of Maya Angelou's semi-autobiographical novel, *I Know Why the Caged Bird Sings*. As she reflected upon the constraints of her own participation in the black experience, and the formative power it had in her life, she finally could understand "why the caged bird sings."[10] That same definition, instead of constraining her, contributed to her impetus to forge a significant future for herself.

One of the dilemmas congregations face is that the selection of designated teachers rarely raises questions concerning the clarity of the good news incarnated in a prospective teacher's message and method. The result is often that some people seeking to clarify the implications of their own commitments end up teaching those exploring the content of those same commitments. That apathy, confusion, and disillusionment are the consequences should not surprise us. The process is evident in the lectures of many teachers, whether in the Sunday church school, or the college or seminary classrooms. Relying primarily upon the words of former teachers, some book or printed resource guide, they seek to enliven and illuminate some past thought or event. Their teaching may hint at the possibilities of its power for our lives, but they have yet to be possessed by it themselves. They are still trying to grasp its implications in a rudimentary fashion. They do not incarnate its depth or breadth. The Gospel of John recognized the importance of this incarnational power. The Word becomes flesh. It dwells among us. That incarnational transformation does not occur as the result of reading the Bible Quarterly, upon certification from some teacher-training event, upon graduation from college or seminary, or by reading through a lesson plan on Saturday night. It occurs only in the focusing of one's commitment to the point that that commitment is revealed in one's attitudes, relationships, and actions.

The teachers who thus incarnate the meanings of the community's past reveal the depth and breadth of some originating event for their students, both in their encounter with the event and with their students. I like J. Stanley Glen's description of Jesus' teaching as the "fleshly spearhead" of the gospel.[11] It underscores my point. The teacher is the point where the meanings central to the insights emerging from the community's significant past make contact with its hoped-for future.

I recognize that the point I am making poses a major dilemma for pastors and leaders of church schools. In one sense I am grateful for that fact. For too long, congregations have relied on people who teach out of a sense of duty, those who have recently joined the fellowship and are anxious to serve the church in some way, or the young adult filled with energy and enthusiasm. The contributions of these people must be taken seriously. Indeed, the first provides continuity in the educational program, and all three may contribute significantly to the relational needs of those with whom they work. As in any setting, some learning may occur, but to call these activities *teaching* stretches the point. The few "teachers" to be found in any congregation are those who have lived and struggled with the claim of the gospel upon their own lives and have responded to the point that its meanings and purposes may be revealed both in what they say and in what they do. These people may be found teaching, whether they have been recruited for the classroom or not. Indeed, they often are not found in the classroom. Instead, they are asked to tell stories at potluck suppers. They provide a theological framework for an issue under discussion during a committee meeting. They reflect on a sermon with others in the parking lot. Their commitment to the significance of the past for the future compels them to convey their insight, wisdom, or skill to others in a wide variety of places. At the same time, others seek them out to clarify an issue, to answer a question, or to interpret the meaning of an event that intrigues or bothers them.

In the second place, *teachers recreate the past to open up the future.* This teaching task reflects again the distinctive relationship of the teacher to the heritage of the community and to those in whom the community's future exists. Three conditions in the teacher's situation prompt this creative act. (1) The vastness of what could be taught requires teachers to order and to choose from the whole field of options available to them. They cannot teach everything they know. The task would engulf them and overwhelm their students. (2) The constantly changing situation we live in alters the way we view and use the knowledge and skill available to us. We cannot assume that what worked yesterday will necessarily be useful today. The teacher must adapt, modify, reconstruct, recast, or create anew from the resources of the past to make relevant those experiences and meanings to our present circumstances. (3) The wide range of methods and strategies available to the teacher to communicate with their students necessitates choosing, not only those approaches sensitive to the students' capacities and interests and the teachers' experience and competence, but also those appropriate to the particular subject and task occupying their attention. Any methodology can give form to the teacher's intent. The effective use of any methodology requires imagination and creativity of the teacher.

Teachers, as mediators between past and future, must constantly choose from the vast resources available to them and recast them for an ever-changing present. In this sense, the teacher's task is not unlike the artist's. In preparing for the moment of interaction with their students, teachers seek to design and structure a new reality. They bring to that exchange a new way of seeing the encounter of meanings from the past with the realities of the present. James Joyce evoked this creative dimension of the teaching act in his affirmation of the role of the artist in society. The artist goes forth each day, said Joyce, "to encounter for the millionth time the reality of experience and to forge in the smithy" of his or her soul "the uncreated conscience" of the race.[12] Hence the teacher trusts the future, even though he or she may despair of the contemporary scene. The teacher is a ray of hope for the possibility of the future in the midst of collapsing institutions and shortsighted leadership. I am sure that many teachers may find the experience of Jeremiah not unlike their own. The leadership has sold out to the prevailing cultural forces. The threat of political chaos and social destruction seems imminent. Those to be taught seem blind and deaf to the truth of their situation. But if teachers succumb to these pressures, they have abdicated their responsibilities. Instead of creatively handing on the resources of the past to forge a new future, they contribute to culture's demise.

The creative act, as Rollo May reminds us, requires tremendous courage.[13] It is not for the weak of mind or heart. In the appropriation and reformulation of the past for an ever-changing present, the teacher creates a new way of seeing, a new way of doing. Whenever teachers act to encourage their students to think with increasing vigor or to act with increasing skill, they contribute to the possibility of disorder. These actions upset the status quo. They threaten the familiar. They may destroy the illusions that guide the lives of many. They may challenge the death perpetuated in sterile and outmoded forms, irrelevant conceptions, and parochial attitudes. They establish new standards or expectations for others.

Perhaps it is this threat to social order that has contributed to the efforts to undermine and control the role of the teacher in our churches and schools. All too often we make them classroom managers, designers of learning experiences and environmental technicians in order to create the illusion that they are engaged in the learning enterprise as teachers; minus, however, the cutting edge crucial to the teacher's role. This cultural captivity of teachers is seen in the repeated expectations that they should be nice, peaceful, loving, gentle, and neutral. The extent of this subjugation of teaching is most evident in the immediate response of a congregation or community when one of their designated teachers broaches an area of controversy. Often this person is dismissed or silenced. These acts deny the very fact that teaching is inherently a controversial activity. It is the result of the soul-searching struggle to effect order in the midst of chaos, to reveal sham and hypocrisy, to uncover superficiality and self-serving interests, and to project visions that might inspire subsequent generations to enrich and enhance the experience of the human race. Each of these actions disrupts even as it clarifies and redirects the life of the community. Teaching is not for the weak-hearted.

Teachers are often made to stand for the past. Parents, community leaders, and congregational members expect them to uphold and perpetuate the ideas, values, and practices they hold dear. This point of view, however, subverts the function of teaching. The authority of teachers, in fact, is not derived from their knowledge about the past, but from the effectiveness with which they recreate those inherited meanings and skills for the present. Consequently a teacher's "teaching" is never *right* in an ultimate or definitive sense. It is always an act in the process of change. Undoubtedly this ambiguity is not one that either many teachers or many members of a society fully appreciate. Desiring to hold on to what they know rather than to participate in its reformulation for the future, they attempt to view the teacher's authority as normative. In the process they create a distance between teacher and learner that is bound to end in failure. When teachers believe that their authority exists in their institutional roles, in their knowledge of the subject matter, or even in their possession of the teacher's guide, the interaction of teacher and learner is diminished. The content of the teacher's commitments is compromised and the student's future is circumscribed.

The teacher's creative act, unlike the artist's, is not simply concerned "with hearing and expressing the vision within his or her own being."[14] Rather, the creative act exists always for someone or a group of someones. Teachers consequently do more than merely incarnate meanings central to the life of the community; they recreate them to be used.

In the third place, *they also re-present them to those entering into and moving through the community.* As indicated earlier, teaching is an action. It involves, in one sense at least, a performance or reenactment of what has been received or recreated. When we teach, we assume the presence of people whose relationship to us is defined by their own relationship to those meanings and experiences. They are novitiates, students, disciples, or pilgrims moving from one level of awareness, one way of understanding or one way of behaving, to another.

Teachers engage in specific activities to facilitate this process. In doing so, they rely on a variety of theories about the nature of teaching and learning. They employ a wide range of methodologies. If one accepts the possibility that quite diverse assumptions regarding the nature and purpose of being human have validity, these theories and approaches to teaching all "work." Teachers teach and people learn in environments governed by pragmatic, behavioristic, humanistic, and existential perspectives. Both the lecture and the open classroom, with its environment of discovery-oriented resources, may facilitate learning.

Because I believe the current focus on teaching behaviors is inadequate for understanding the nature and significance of teaching, I find myself asking what it is that the community must do to incorporate the young, the immigrant and the convert into its way of seeing, believing, and doing. This does not mean that I ignore the insights of those who approach teaching from what is clearly a social science perspective, as do John B. Hough and James K. Duncan or James Michael Lee.[15] On the contrary, their work may well refine and sharpen the approach to the teaching task I am suggesting. But I needed a perspective that would help me understand why our teaching so often involves episodic as well as structured events, intuitive as well as rational responses, and destructive as well as creative actions.

The results of teaching are not necessarily rational or progressive. A person encountering new ways of perceiving, thinking, or doing must often go through a period of "unlearning." Disorientation, pain, isolation, confusion, and anxiety must be included with excitement, a growing sense of competence, and confidence as signs that people are engaged in the learning process.

Teaching does not simply build upon previous knowledge and experience. Instead, teaching always involves a negative act. It calls into judgment our current understandings, actions and feelings. There is more to do and to know. There are additional skills to develop. There are new ways to behave. In re-presenting meanings and skills of the community, teachers often confront what Rollo May has called "the actual (as contrasted with ideal) gods of our society."[16] Any such battle is rarely orderly, peaceful, or rational. It involves challenge and courage. It may lead to disappointment, disillusionment, and even despair. It may be exhilarating. It is always demanding. The re-presentation of the life and meanings of the community is never easy, because it involves both responsibility for the heritage of the community and sensitivity to the student in whom the future of the community exists.

In the presentation of the life and meanings of the community, teachers do engage in at least seven distinctive tasks. The first four reflect the teacher's relationship to the community's expectations. The remaining three tasks point to the responsibility teachers have for communicating with people with sensitivity. It is obvious that, in any formal or informal teaching-learning event, teachers may employ several of these functions at the same time.

The Tasks of Teachers as Representatives of the Community

Teachers deliberately *seek to transmit the past into the present.* Although people are often unaware of the processes of transmission they use to induct the young and the immigrant into their midst, the self-conscious community never trusts the handing on of traditions, customs, rituals, attitudes, morals, or values to chance.

The processes of transmission have been most carefully

explored by anthropologists. Margaret Mead, for example, observed they occur whenever a people "depends for continuity upon the expectations of the old and upon the almost ineradicable imprint of those expectations upon the young." In slowly changing cultures, "it depends upon the adults' being able to see the parents who reared them, as they rear their own children in the way they themselves were reared."[17] The possibility of discerning the continuity of both the goals of one's teaching and the way one teaches across three generations keeps the expectations of the community very clear. In rapidly changing societies, however, the process is often disjointed unless it is undertaken with explicit and conscious efforts to hand on what has been received.

This process is most evident in what educators have long called *indoctrination*. Unfortunately, through misuse and a misunderstanding of its critical function in maintaining the identity of a community across time, the term, for educators, has acquired pejorative connotations. Indeed, very few contemporary books on teaching make any use of the word at all. And yet, as Locke Bowman rightly observes, "if we say that we do not indoctrinate, we deceive ourselves." For Bowman, indoctrination means "to imbue with ideas, opinions, and formulas for believing and acting." It involves a culturally accepted form of "interpretation, approved and passed on for the benefit of the community."[18]

Many of the resources for the transmission of those central "ideas, opinions, and formulas" in any community are to be found in the stories, songs, images, symbols, and rituals that fill the daily lives of people. These resources for the common life of the community are often so familiar to us we are not aware of their significance. Their importance, however, cannot be underestimated. They introduce us to mysteries in life that cannot be contained in logical discourse or rational formulas. They enrich our imaginations and provide the building blocks for our creative activity. They link us to meanings that are rooted in the past but have the power to transform our future. They intensify our identification with the experience of a given people in a particular place. They influence our expectations of ourselves and of those who live in different communities with different stories, songs, images, symbols, and rituals.

We may see the effect of these resources in the memorized prayers, creeds, and hymns congregations use to express their particular experience with the mystery of the divine. They may be seen in the prejudices and value judgments that distinguish the members of one group from the members of another. They are evident in the heroes, heroines, and saints the people of one group hold up as models for their personal and corporate lives. They are to be found in the continuity of certain behavioral responses—standing or kneeling automatically during prayer, the handshake of the American or the bow of the Japanese upon greeting another person, or the "right" way to hold a fork during dinner. They are revealed in the power of certain symbols to rivet the attention, arouse the passion, and influence the actions of men and women in the routines of daily life, as well as in those critical moments when the identity or continuity of the community is being challenged.

The transmission of the heritage of the community through both conscious and unconscious patterns of indoctrination is crucial to the continuity of the life and identity of the community. It is the means whereby that which is of "deepest value to a community" is set "firmly in the minds"[19] and actions of its members. It is the way we appropriate most of the liturgical resources we use in celebrating our church, lodge, ethnic, or national commitments. It is the means through which most of us learned the basic social graces—how to sing "Happy Birthday to You" and "Jesus Loves Me," to recite the Lord's Prayer, or how to behave in the manner deemed appropriate for a man or a woman in our culture. Much of this is taught by "precept and admonition." Edwin T. Hall has observed that such indoctrination often occurs when an "adult mentor molds the young according to patterns" he or she has never questioned. Such teaching often takes place "when a mistake is made and someone corrects it," usually without explanation.[20] Indoctrination puts limits on our responses. We are shown that there is a "right" way to do certain tasks, to think, to perceive in relation to the commitments and values of the community of which we are a part. That "right" way is subsequently at work in our ability to distinguish the members of one group from another by the way they speak, act, dress, worship, perhaps even raise their children or treat their aged.

Much of the resistance to transmissive forms of teaching among educators may be traced to the autocratic character of much school teaching. But most of our common experience with modes of indoctrination does not occur in schools. Rather, it is most frequently used in familial and other non-school settings. People of all ages can be found playing this transmissive role. Children, especially, engage in transmissive teaching. Among the most intriguing aspects of our cultural life are the games handed down for generations from older children to younger children. Some, for example, can be traced back to the Middle Ages with few changes in their rules. Such is the persistent power of children's efforts in teaching children.

Indoctrination takes place in predominantly unconscious modes in relatively stable and secure societies. When the identity of a people is threatened by minority status or external influences, however, efforts to transmit characteristic behaviors, attitudes, values, and perspectives from one generation to the next are made with increasing intentionality. Perhaps the strength of the Jewish community throughout the world can be traced, in part, to their extensive efforts to imbue succeeding generations with the character and meaning of being Jewish. Those of us who are both American and Christian have not, until recently, been particularly concerned with extending our corporate identity into the future. Unlike our Jewish neighbors, we could assume that the relatively unconscious patterns of enculturation would introduce the next generation into an American and Christian way of life. With the increasing secularization of our own society, the accessibility of other religious and cultural patterns from around the world, and the challenge of technological value systems, we no longer have that luxury. As a people, we are faced increasingly with the necessity of deciding what those who are just entering our common life must know and do to extend our corporate identity into the future. In the past, we have often been put off by the autocratic character of particular transmissive modes of education. When they are inhumane, they should be challenged. But as a mode for teaching in a rapidly changing world, indoctrination is one of the central ways a community provides continuity for its members.

Teachers instruct that people might be guided by the values, practices, and commitments of the community. Instruction not only has to do with the inculcation of precepts and ideas: it is primarily concerned, as James Michael Lee has emphasized, with the learners' lifestyle. The most significant concern of the teacher will be the consistency of the learners' responses to life with the vision, the faith, and the practices of the community. Through instruction, teachers give direction to the ways people organize their experience.

Instruction is, consequently, an intentional activity intruding upon the vicissitudes of a person's growth with the expectations and disciplines of the community. It need not be dogmatic. The word *instruction* has also received bad press due to the tendency of teachers to equate it with predominately verbal and authoritarian behaviors. Jerome Bruner, on the contrary, emphasizes that instruction gives a person a predisposition to learning. It should structure potential learnings so they might be readily grasped. Instruction should create sequences through which people can grasp the issues, ideas, and skills required to master the task or subject. It should specify "the nature and pacing of rewards and punishments in the process of learning and teaching."[21]

Almost any methodology may employ Bruner's theory. The point is that instruction involves a controlled process whereby those being taught may appropriate the resources and disciplines considered central to the ongoing life of the community. Through instruction, teachers emphasize the significance of skills for perceiving, thinking, and acting in ways that perpetuate the values, commitments, and lifestyles of the community. Instruction, in other words, takes the notion seriously that people must be able to identify with the values and practices of the community before they can be empowered to participate in its life.

In the context of the community, instruction should do more than dispose people to learn. It should contribute to the formation of their identity. Instruction is central to the task of entering into the life of the community because it is concerned with the consistency between the values, commitments, and lifestyle of the one being taught and those espoused and practiced by the community. This point of view undergirds the rationale for the "instruction" of converts before they accept the vows of membership in the community. Our nation does not allow immigrants immediate, full rights of citizenship. They must first engage in an educational process and participate in the life of the nation that they might become citizens, not only in name, but in the way they see and respond to life. Churches similarly require converts, even baptized people transferring membership from one congregation to another, to go to catechism or participate in "membership classes." These periods of instruction are crucial both for the people entering the congregation and for the congregation itself. What the outsider or newcomer learns provides the basis for incorporating him or her into the fellowship of the congregation. Their learnings renew, at the same time, the congregation's vision and life through the vitality of the new members' commitment. Instruction, especially for people standing on a threshold during their personal or corporate pilgrimage, is a second thing teachers do in and for the community.

Teachers mediate for people caught up in the immediacy of the present the offensive character of the truth and wisdom in the community's heritage. Teaching punctures illusions and reveals the presence of hypocrisy. It opens up untested assumptions to reveal their superficiality or wrongness. It confronts our ignorance and incompetence. It unmasks the false gods that hold our allegiance. It penetrates the "mystification" that cloaks the experience of vast numbers of people who feel so completely at home with their situation that they do not recognize their own estrangement and alienation. A pastor friend of mine often described this process as one of helping affluent Americans discover the nature of their own hunger, which heretofore they rarely recognized or acknowledged.

J. Stanley Glen clearly described the task of mediating the offense that characterizes the teacher's role by saying that the source of this responsibility is in the teacher's concern for particularity and integrity. The teacher consistently asks questions about the faithfulness of a given thought or practice to the intent of the community's life. This question of historical relevance is balanced by a corresponding question about the ethics of people's responses. Glen observes that "a teacher is always a judge." The teacher makes demands upon those they teach, places obligations on them, asks questions that cut to the core of their being.[22] In so doing, teachers often disrupt the flow of their lives.

Greene describes the process somewhat differently. Teachers "combat" the illusions that often govern our lives by a vigorous critique of what appears to be natural, but is in fact no more than a construction of social reality. This "wide-awakeness," she believes, is a crucial consequence of the interrelation of teacher and learner. It is important "not only for the sake of overcoming ignorance and warding off manipulations, but in order to resist the cynicism and powerlessness that silence as they paralyse."[23]

A boy's candid observation that the emperor had no clothes (in the popular fairy story) may illustrate something of the teacher's function of criticizing and bringing judgment upon the illusions, mystifications, hypocrisies, and untested assumptions that govern our perceptions and actions. Greene observes that he engaged in what Paul Ricouer has called "a more authentic speaking."[24]

Such authentic speaking characterized much of the teaching of Jesus. His words and actions often penetrated, with unsparing insight, the rationalizations and superficial piety of his contemporaries. He held up the example of the despised

Samaritan as a model of neighborliness. He told the
law-abiding man to sell his prized possessions if he desired
eternal life. He saw in children the meaning of being faithful.
He ate with lepers and sinners. He envisioned the sustaining
love and care of God for the disfranchised and dispossessed,
and foresaw eternal torment for the comfortable and powerful.
Such teaching created much pain and anguish, both for the
disciples and for many in the crowds surrounding him.

Teaching, consequently, does not always culminate in
pleasant growing experiences as the handbooks for teachers
often imply. Rather, if teaching is faithful to the community's
experience, it always raises critical questions about the integrity
and purpose of contemporary thought and action. This task is
crucial if teaching is to serve as a link between the community's
past and its future. It is critical if our teaching is not to settle into
a preoccupation with instructional strategies and learning
environments. And it is critical to the task of purging our
contemporary experiences of pretense and illusion. In short, it
is the indispensable prerequisite for making sense out of those
experiences.

*Teachers interpret meanings and experiences from the past for
a new generation in a new situation.* Interpretation involves the
creation of relationships out of the continuities and incongrui-
ties to be found in the interplay of resources inherited from the
past, and current events and circumstances. James Smart points
out that the task of interpretation begins "before we are
conscious of doing anything other" than reading the words or
recalling the circumstances surrounding the thought and events
from the past. We hear words and we perceive events in "the
total context of our present historical existence"[25]—a context
that, for many of us, has changed several times during our
lifetime.

The context is general, in that we share its basic features
with others. We can provide labels and generalizations—
conservative, liberal, Methodist, Catholic, black, native
American—to indicate certain commonalities. But we also
approach the past out of the distinctive framework of our

personal perceptions and experience—a context uniquely one's own. For example, my boyhood church environment lifted into my consciousness the power of the example of Jesus as a model for our lives. During seminary on the edge of Harlem in the middle of the civil rights movement, my new context brought to my attention the liberating themes in the life and message of Jesus the Christ. The personal pain of many people in my first parish allowed me to hear the healing and reconciling words at the heart of his ministry. In recent years, growing sensitivity to the disparity between the commitments integral to the life centered on Christ and those caught up in the civil religion of many church members has led me to a new appreciation for the demands of discipleship to a master who has penetrated the mystery of death in many different forms. Each context has made it possible to see the Christ figure in new and perhaps more comprehensive ways.

James Sanders reminds us that the task of interpretation involves more than comprehending both contexts. It has to do with the translation of "a thought or event from one cultural context . . . to another."[26] The teacher as interpreter functions as a telescope opening up the particularities and mysteries of the past to reveal the hidden dimensions of our contemporary experience. On the one hand, this task involves the use of all the research skills and theoretical insights available to us for exploring the situation, the actions, the thought, the values, and the commitments of some given event in our heritage. At the same time, it demands that we use contemporary language, art forms, concepts, and constructs that the wisdom and experience of the past might be made usable today. The teacher brings up to date, if you will, the collective meanings of the human race, without, at the same time, distorting them for contemporary ends.

Hence, interpretation expands our awareness of our connectedness with the totality of human experience. We become increasingly conscious of our mutuality across both time and space.[27] Black people's identification of their pilgrimage from slavery to emancipation with the Hebrews' exodus from the Egyptian slave camps to the promised land illustrates that the common themes of existence are not bound by the structures of time. The Bible often comes alive for people when they first discover that it is not an ancient book describing the interactions of God and a group of people in the long ago. Rather it is an ancient book that reveals to us our involvement in the story of God's persistent love for all people in all ages and places, including here and now. The exile, the return to Jerusalem, the call of the disciples, the fragile finitude of the early churches not only existed back then, but are a daily part of our own lives. This growing consciousness not only reveals our connectedness with the total human experience, but it clarifies the distinctions between our experience and that of others. The exodus of the Hebrews and the pilgrimage of the American blacks were not the same events. Our own denials of Jesus Christ are not simply the repetition of Peter's. Our words of praise are set in a different context from those of the psalmists. Our valleys of the shadow of death contain dangers unknown to our ancestors. We are not simply an extension of our past. We make choices from what we have received. And we are responsible to ourselves, to our neighbors and to God for the content and consequences of those choices. We not only judge the experiences of the past; we are judged by the use we make of these experiences.

Interpretation expands our awareness of our connectedness with the totality of human experience. We become increasingly conscious of our mutuality across both time and space. At the same time, through interpretation, we also integrate and make coherent the diffuse elements of our increasing knowledge. We pull the disparate strands of discrete information into coherent wholes. We begin to discern, not only our connectedness, but the overarching themes and forces binding together the experience of all humanity. We ground the emerging meanings in symbolic expressions because we discover that the whole is greater than the parts we are able to identify and describe. We use symbols that are increasingly power-full for us. They grab our attention. They focus our commitments. They compel us to act. Our relationship to them begins to clarify who we are and to locate us in the mainstream of history.

The cross, for example, is simply an instrument of torture and death. Thousands of people died upon crosses. Functionally, it has no more meaning and power than a host of ancient and modern implements used for socially approved murder. As the means of the death of Jesus of Nazareth, the one called Jesus the Christ, Son of God, the cross takes on a significance for Christians transcending its utilitarian function. The cross gathers up numerous disparate themes in the Jewish tradition and unifies them in a symbolic whole. The cross becomes the means by which a growing band of people down through the centuries began to understand the extent of the steadfast love of God, the character of sacrificial love, the quality of judgment experienced as forgiveness, and the power of the forces of life to penetrate and overcome the finality of death—themes running throughout the Old Testament record. The cross becomes a powerful expression of their unity. It has since served as the rallying point for millions of people throughout the ages. It became, not an instrument of torture, but a source of our corporate identity. We live in its shadow as the people of the cross.

The power of the cross in our lives, however, is made available to us in the rhythmic interplay of opening up the varieties of its meanings in the hidden recesses of our corporate past and gathering those meanings into coherent wholes. The process of differentiating and expanding meanings on the one hand, and of integrating and unifying them on the other, is basic to the teacher's task. The teacher who does not embrace this awesome responsibility of interpreting the human experience does worse than merely prevent his or her students from enjoying the riches of their heritage. Such a teacher keeps them from making informed decisions about their futures.

The Tasks of Teachers as Agents of the Future

In the rhythmic interplay of those entering and engaging the events and meanings of a community, the teacher's responsi-

bility to the community is balanced by the teacher's responsiveness to the children, youth, and/or adults being taught.
Knowledge of their intellectual, spiritual and physical capacities, awareness of their interests, and sensitivity to their needs
become crucial building blocks in the teacher's efforts to
recreate and represent the life and meanings of the community
for those entering it. These issues have dominated the attention
of educators during the last several decades. Their research is
extensive and their writing is voluminous. We now know much
more about the people we call learners or students, but I am still
just as impressed by the extent of what we do not know. The
resulting complexity and confusion do not make it easy to
identify three or four characteristics of the teacher who is
responsive to the personal and corporate learning needs of
those entering or working their way toward full identification
with the life of the community of faith. Yet I find that teachers
who both effectively reflect the character of those who respond
with a commitment to the future of the community, and have a
corresponding sensitivity to those they teach, do at least three
things.

*Teachers with a commitment to the community's future are
present to those they teach.* They share in the rhythmic patterns
of their students' daily lives. The sensitive teacher is not an
outsider or a stranger to their worlds, but is a fellow traveler. In
their life together, teachers begin to discern the distinctive ways
that the generalized categories of the developmentalists,
educators, and other social scientists are specifically expressed
in the thinking and doing of their students. They become
sensitive to the contexts out of which they respond to the
pressures and demands of life in its physical, social, and
spiritual dimensions.

I am reminded of a church school teacher known by parents
and children alike as one who was present to them. She planned
for each session. She missed a session only when she was sick or
on vacation. She spent time with all the children in their
respective homes. She talked with their parents. In some cases
she met with their public school teachers. She kept a record of

birthdays and sent cards. She listened for special events in their lives and acknowledged these events in her conversations, celebrated them in moments of worship, and allowed them to influence her teaching plans and activities. She kept notes on some of the children to remind herself of their special interests, abilities, and concerns. She sought, in other words, to get in touch with their lives. Within the limits of her time and energy and the structures of the church school, she was present to those she taught.

Teachers who are present to those they teach are persistent. They do not abandon their students even when they appear to have wandered astray. Jesus' experience in Gethsemane is one with which teachers are familiar. Effective plans, significant personal relationships, even the fear of punishment cannot consistently hold the attention of those they teach. They fall asleep. They wander away like lost sheep. They often turn on the teacher when they are filled with disappointment, mistrust or anger. They giggle and goof off. They appear distracted and are easily tempted to follow other "teachers." In spite of their tendency to do so, teachers cannot prevent or even control such responses. Instead, they search for those who are lost. They follow up on absentees. They forgive those who disappoint them. They embrace those who have placed false hopes in them. They carry burdens for those too weak to shoulder them alone.

Teachers who are present are compassionate. They recognize the finitude of people but do not hold it against them. Their teaching is distinguished by its ethical sensitivity to the moral issues involved in the teacher-learner relationship. They do not confuse their authority with the power to control or manipulate the minds or spirits of those they teach. They exercise judgment with restraint. They are just and gracious. They approach their students with sensitivity to the differences among them, yet with impartiality in acknowledging their students' respective gifts and talents.

Teachers who are present to those they teach can see the future in and through their students. Jesus approached the final days of his ministry, not with a sense of the things left undone, but with an awareness that he had fulfilled his mission. His work would not cease. Through the disciples it would be continued. In a similar fashion a teacher may see, in a teenager struggling to understand where a biblical passage and a contemporary event intersect, the capacity to proclaim and interpret the gospel. Through a young child's prayer, a teacher may discern the potential for a life that will mediate the graciousness of God's mercy. In an adult's frustration over inequities in the marketplace, a teacher may envision a future advocate of justice and righteousness. Seeing the future in our students implies that we are able to see potential for people's futures in their actions now. When teachers encourage the development of that potential, their students may approach the future with anticipation and purposefulness.

Teachers committed to the community's future "activate" the learning of those they teach. Activate is the word Locke Bowman uses to describe the nature of teaching. Teaching, he observes, causes "something important to begin, in the full recognition that one is not wholly responsible for what went before and for what will come."[28] Teaching initiates an action. It elicits a response. It provokes thought. It plays a catalytic function in the life of the learner. It leads people through complex issues and concepts.

To activate learning, teachers perform the tasks described earlier—transmitting, instructing, mediating, and interpreting. These tasks, however, must now be ordered in a way that facilitates learning. Teachers activate learning by first creating environments that will motivate personal interest and respond to human needs. Some environments are easily staged. "Once upon a time" is an ancient formula for beginning a story. It sets the framework for a teacher-learner interaction that is often highly charged with interest or expectation. Other environments are more complex. Much attention has been given in recent years to the importance of a richly endowed setting for the work of students in schools. This interest, however, has a long history. The educational reformers of the nineteenth century underscored the value of a variety of resources to aid learning. John Dewey and Maria Montessori, from their different perspectives, stressed the potential for students' learning more when they can actually be engaged in exploring the properties, limits and possibilities of the subject or task at hand. The open classroom and the increased popularity of the media in educational settings reflect educators' continuing recognition of the power of an enriched environment to activate learning responses in students.

Teachers also activate learning with strategies that engage people at the edges of their capacities, interests, and needs. Jerome Bruner, as mentioned earlier, calls this process cultivating in people a "predisposition to learning." In simpler terms, teachers engage learners at the growth edges of their lives.

When teachers are sensitive to these growth edges, they first look for what their students already know and can do. No one enters a new situation without some prior experience that helps one organize any new information, assess its importance, and select the parts that may be useful in the future. The disparity between prior experiences and new expectations provides a distinctive opportunity for the teacher to work. The interest people have in their familiar past, as well as the vulnerability and defenselessness they experience in a setting where old ways of thinking and acting appear to be dysfunctional, provide the occasion for sensitive teaching. When people are open to new possibilities and are searching for clues about how to make sense out of a new situation, they are often looking for a guide. At this point, their teachers may open up the new context by helping them make connections with their previous experiences. The author of the second part of the book of Isaiah fulfilled this task for the Jews in Babylon. In powerful language, this writer helped the people in a strange land see that they were still a chosen people, but with an expanded mission. School teachers attempt to make these connections during the beginning of each school year with a review of the past that points to the goals and tasks of the new year. The effective teacher persists in this task throughout the teacher-learner relationship.

Learners also bring to each new situation some ability to make sense out of it. The research of Piaget, Kohlberg, Fowler, and others underscores the developmental character of this ability. When taken seriously, their insights help teachers recognize that the young child does not hear the story of the Good Samaritan in the same way that a teenager or an older adult might hear it. All three may have the capacity to repeat the teacher's words verbatim. But if asked to put the story into their own words, they would tell quite different versions. The story would be influenced by the varying extent of their ability to conceptualize abstract ideas and relationships, to see the significance of the story for their own lives, and to view its implications for the actions of people in general.

The variation in people's capacity for understanding was made vivid for me in a conversation between a church school teacher and a four-year-old about the meaning of the Golden Rule. No matter how the teacher phrased her question, the young boy insisted that it meant that, if a playmate should hit him first, it would be all right to return the punch. If, in a moment of anger or frustration, he should first hit his friend, it would be wrong for the friend to hit him back. Erikson would not have been surprised at this response. The young child's developmental concerns center more on autonomy than on reciprocity in relationships. This fact influences everything he or she might say or do, including the way she or he might appropriate the meaning of this common biblical passage. Sensitivity to these developmental differences can help teachers make decisions about what to do with a given body of material or a given task for the persons they teach.

Educators have increasingly tended to use the insights of the developmentalists to arrange bodies of knowledge into sequences appropriate to the capacities of a given age group. Although these efforts may be helpful, they have all too often become artificial and arbitrary. Their judgments have been accepted as normative rather than suggestive. One of the most obvious consequences may be seen in church-school resources that limit children's access to the total biblical narrative. "In our haste to protect children from the harsher details of some of the Biblical accounts" on the basis of some developmental criteria, as Locke Bowman notes, we may, consequently, "be depriving them of just the furnishings of mind they need in order to sense the Scriptures' way of speaking directly to life as it really is."[29] We forget, in other words, that the insights of the developmentalists are apt to be more helpful in discerning what people of varying ages may do with their experiences in an educational situation, than they are to be helpful in choosing educational activities and tasks for them. In almost every group of people, there are some whose behavior simply does not fit the generalized description of the capacities that may be characteristic of the potential in their respective age groups. In short, the approach of the developmentalists, which has dominated the recent efforts of curriculum writers and many teachers, often ignores both the limited nature of developmental research and the complexity of factors that make up the growth edges of any group of people.

Teachers, to be sensitive to their students' ability to learn, must also be aware of the interests of those they teach. People are not abstract creatures. They come in very concrete shapes and forms, with established networks of relationships and active value systems. The child who values solitude is not very open to intensive group learning activities. The boy who perceives the church to be "for women" may not feel comfortable in the church school, especially if his only significant encounters with adults in the church are with women. The teenager who longs to have an active social life may not want to take part in a youth group that is primarily involved in study and mission. Sensitivity to such interests provides teachers with some of the clues they need to engage their students in a learning task.

Teachers also activate learning by being clear about what the community wants or needs from its initiates. The coach of an athletic team recognizes this fact clearly. If someone wants to be a member of the football team, that person must develop certain skills, understand certain maneuvers, and achieve a certain level of competence. Musical organizations, fraternities and sororities, and many lodges and service clubs state with similar clarity what they need and expect from their members.

Historically, confirmation has functioned in a similar manner in the church. There are certain things one must know, certain disciplines with which one should be familiar, certain expectations one must meet prior to the community's acceptance of one's intention to identify with it. During the last several years, the declaration of the community's expectations of students in the church has been confused by the tendency of educators to draw their clues about learning primarily from the ways people learn and grow. Teachers have been urged to help their students explore the life and mission of the church but they have not been encouraged to involve those same students in that life and mission.

When working with church-school teachers, pastors, and congregational committees on education, I usually ask what they want people to know, what they want them to be able to do, and what attitudes they would like people to have about themselves, the church, and the world after twelve to fifteen years of involvement in the congregation. I have yet to be in a congregation where its leaders can begin to answer that question with any clarity or specificity. I believe that some of the apathy we see in many congregations is due to this void. Similarly, the lack of enthusiasm in many teachers may well be traced to their sense of being technicians who facilitate the goals and interests of their students, rather than being representatives of the community who are expected to engage those interests with the values, commitments, and practices of the community.

Teachers committed to the community's future also become learners to their students' teaching. The consequence of any teaching act is the reformulation and representation of that event by learners. It is organized in a fresh way. It is ordered in relation to their own perceptions, capacities and experiences. It

145

is made new. The opportunity for teachers to learn from their students usually happens when teachers give tests. When teachers see those occasions only as times to test or measure a student's progress, they diminish the importance of the give-and-take of the teaching-learning interaction. They perpetuate the image of the teacher as one who funnels knowledge into the student. They do not see themselves as recipients of their students' insights. When a person refuses to be confined by this arrangement and insists on sharing his or her perceptions and insights, such teachers are often as astounded with a learner's knowledge or skill as the priests and rabbis were when they listened to the young Jesus. We, too, may well be amazed at the perceptive insights coming from the "mouths of babes." Sensitive teachers recognize that in any teaching-learning interaction they may be led by a child or the neophyte. That fact does not change the necessity for the wise, knowledgeable and skilled in the community to teach. It only underscores the fact that the roles in any teaching-learning relationship are always subject to change. In this sense the teaching-learning interaction may be considered to be dialogical. Learning may often be activated by teachers, but that same learning may initiate some new insight or understanding for the teacher. As the writers of the later portions of Isaiah reveal, they so knew and understood those teachings that they could "update" them for a new age and situation. In the immediacy of the continuing relationship of teachers and learners, this dialogical process keeps the former alert and growing. It also allows the latter to perceive that (even if in a rudimentary form) they also contribute to the thinking and doing of the community.

Summary

In this chapter, I have explored with you what it means for the community of faith to take teaching seriously. I have taken the position that teaching is one of the functions the community employs to introduce people into its life and to help them move to increasingly deeper levels of commitment, understanding, and participation. To that end, the designated teachers of the community systematically (and others informally) incarnate the meanings of the community, that their students may encounter them directly. They recreate the heritage of the community that those they teach may encounter it in ways appropriate to their experience, interest, and ability. They re-present those resources and meanings so that their students may explore them to the end that they may begin to identify with the community and participate in shaping its future. The importance of these tasks calls for people with special gifts and graces embodied in clear commitments and sensitive relationships with students. The task of teachers is demanding. It is audacious. But it is also necessary, if the heritage that has nurtured us for the present is to help shape the future through the lives of our descendents.

THE LIMITS OF TEACHING IN A CHANGING CONTEXT

The what and how of teaching newcomers in the community is clearest for those who live in a stable and slowly changing world. When the elders of the community are able to envision a world for their children that is, in reality, the perpetuation of their own experience, they know what skills and knowledge are requisite both for survival and for purposeful living. They assume that what works today will also work tomorrow. To teach, for them, is simply to hand on to the next generation what has given life its sustenance and meaning in the present.

Continuity and stability do not describe our world. Even in relatively isolated corners of the world, the forces of change chip away at the authority of tradition and loosen the ties binding generation to generation. It is difficult for the elders of the community to prepare the next generation for a future that they also do not know. Perhaps it is this loss of the community's—and the teacher's—sense of the future that has contributed to the contemporary educator's fascination with playthings of the present moment—teaching strategies and leadership theories and practice. The commitment of most educators to an evolving human future has given teachers license to concentrate on whatever procedures and resources might facilitate personal and corporate growth. The facile acceptance of the latest fads in general education, developmental psychology, and learning theory underscores my point. With little discussion, for example, the developmental categories of Havighurst, Erikson, Piaget, Kohlberg, and Fowler have all too often been incorporated into church-school curriculum designs. Team teaching, open classrooms, intergenerational education, and learning centers have been introduced into the educational programs of many congregations. Churches have used social science categories for leadership in teacher-training programs without questioning or clarifying the impact these structures might have on their commitments. The list is extensive. Much good has come from the adoption of such theories and insights from the social sciences. But the uncritical way they have been accepted and used by all too many church leaders should be questioned.

Underlying this acceptance of social science theories is the assumption that biological evolution has its corollary both in social and spiritual evolution. Just as the strongest might survive in nature (so this view goes), so might the most virtuous endure in society and the most faithful in the kingdom of God. New knowledge, new ways of doing things, new facilities and resources are thereby perceived to be more relevant than the old. Interestingly, this assumption permeates the work of both liberal and conservative educators. Their differences increasingly focus on doctrinal, and not on methodological, matters. This view, unfortunately, tends to equate strength and virtue with faithfulness. It does not account for the reality of sin, which may transform the best intentions into instruments of evil and destruction. It does not account for the subtlety of the spirit-destroying forces permeating contemporary life in forms that would have been unimaginable to our ancestors. It does not account for the failure of our institutions and programs to create moral and faithful citizens. It does not account for battered children in affluent American homes or starving children throughout the world. If we are honest, we must admit that all our efforts, buildings, and programs, while helpful in many respects, simply have not eradicated hunger, discrimination, racism, dishonesty, and a host of other evils contrary to the just and righteous society envisioned as the goal of our Jewish and Christian heritage.

So, as I approach what it means for us in the church to teach, I believe we need to approach our task humbly, acknowledging the limits of our efforts. The arrogance of much Western-European and American teaching is no longer justified. We need to recognize the limitations of our structures. We need to acknowledge that, in the teaching-learning interaction, both teacher and learner have a responsibility, but that it is not a responsibility *for* each other. Their responsibilty is for the way each relates to the community that serves as source, context, and goal of her or his life. As I reflect on what it means for the church (as one community of faith in our complex world) to teach, my own expectations are informed and tempered by several assumptions.

Perhaps one of the most awesome discoveries for those who teach is the recognition that *what we teach may have value today but may not be useful tomorrow.* The rapidity of the changes in our world quickly reveals the finitude of our analyses, our interpretations, and our directions for applying insights from past events for contemporary experiences. The arrogance that for too long has characterized the educational elite in our land no longer has any clout. We find ourselves living as strangers in what we thought was our native land. We think we know where we are and where we are headed, but in fact, the landscape seems to shift before our eyes. We think that continuity is a major characteristic of our common life, but we regularly find ourselves feeling isolated in familiar surroundings. In her provocative study of culture and commitment, Margaret Mead so describes the contemporary older generation. Only the young, familiar with the terrain of rapid change, live as natives in the land. Mead places the dividing line between the older stranger and the young native in 1945, with the bombing of Nagasaki and Hiroshima. Those born since that date have little comprehension of life in a world without the threat of nuclear destruction. Those of us born before that date, she claims, still find ourselves making decisions about our future as if we did not possess that ultimately destructive power. We only delude ourselves in our efforts to perpetuate patterns of relating to others around the world with assumptions grounded in the pre-atomic bomb era.

Mead's designation of that date, however, is too simple. The successful landing made by Neil Armstrong on the moon has expanded our geographic boundaries to unknown limits. The experience of looking upon earth, on television and in the news magazines, as just another planet orbiting around the sun provides a radical shift in perspective from the way we have traditionally viewed ourselves. The earth, for the space-age generation, no longer functions as the center of the universe. Indeed, science fiction scenarios of the future often do not even see it as the center of human activity. That option never before existed for the human race. The changes this event will precipitate undoubtedly will alter the course of human history even more profoundly than the European discovery of the Americas.

Other landmark events will also alter the perceptions and responses of our children to their heritage. The shift in the balance of world power, from those with industrial might to those with energy resources or to those with the capability of producing life in laboratories or manipulating the future of the human race by genetic means, will be among the events altering the way future generations appropriate and use our teaching. An overview of the changes still ahead of us reminds us that we cannot prevent the unfolding of a future we do not comprehend. Our successors will have to choose how to respond to each radical intervention into life as it occurs. Those decisions will include an assessment of our own faithfulness and relevance to our heritage as we have sought to respond to present-day issues and current situations. It is in our faithfulness to that task that our teaching may be useful for the future.

When we teach, we cannot assume that the primary faith decisions of those we teach will center on serving Jesus Christ as lord and master. Neither can we assume that their secondary faith decisions will focus upon choosing among Lutheran, Catholic, Baptist, or Presbyterian communities as the context for the nurture of their faith. Instead, those we teach will be faced with choosing from a variety of faiths. For the first time in our nation's history, Islam, Hinduism, Buddhism, and other great religions of the world provide lively alternatives for many people. They exist no longer as exotic belief systems in distant lands, but as dynamic communities in many of our own cities. Religious affiliation now involves more than decisions between infant's and believer's baptism, historic and normative creeds, formal and informal liturgy, and the like. It has to do with which events of the past will become organizing centers for our decisions and our view of the future. Will we choose the Christ event or the Buddha pilgrimage? Will we be following teachings from Saudi Arabia or India? Or will we gather up elements of several such events? These choices are rarely clear-cut. But they are being made in our churches now. I am intrigued, for example, by the rather common acceptance of reincarnation as a basic doctrine of belief by some of the midwestern, conservative Protestants I have met. In spite of their supposed familiarity with the Bible, I have found that many of these people are unaware that the sources for this belief are not to be found in the Bible. They are surprised to discover that its roots are in religious traditions with which they have little familiarity. My hunch is that they, and we, have little awareness of the effectiveness of the mass media, not only in introducing people to this way of viewing life and its purpose, but also in inclining them to embrace attitudes, values, and practices heretofore considered alien to our own traditions and heritage.

Even more significant for the teacher in the church, however, are the many options in our society that serve as the center of our commitments and influence our actions. Some are related to the theory and practice of our economic system, to our national or political life, or to the media itself. Still others are caught up in events of ethnic and cultural pride; or some common cause such as ecology, disarmament, abortion rights, or the "right to life." Still others reflect the concerns of particular "lifestyles," or the patterning of the stars. Each of these commitments places a demand on our lives. Each exacts some form of loyalty that may or may not be consistent with the values emerging from our own Jewish and Christian heritage.

Teachers simply cannot expect to mold the responses of those they teach. Even in the most isolated communities, alternative perspectives may well attract the attention of many. Again, in this situation, it is my assumption that our task is not to attempt to control the responses of our students, but to seek to make viable the commitments that inform our own teaching.

When we teach, *we cannot assume, moreover, that our teaching is reinforced by the daily life of a given congregation or of the Christian community at large.* Although it may never have worked, mainstream Protestant pastors and teachers have, for the most part, assumed that their efforts were made in a network of mutually interdependent functions of church and community life. Parents, pastors, public school teachers, civic leaders, and church school teachers shared in a common venture with similar goals and expectations. With the exception of several highly self-conscious congregations, we can no longer approach the educational responsibilities of the church with this assumption. The worship and educational efforts of many congregations have little in common. Indeed, they often use different, even contradictory, hymn books and translations of the Bible. Parental involvement in intentional Christian teaching is far from a reality. The partnership of the public and the Sunday school, as Robert W. Lynn has described it, has collapsed. This fact may be seen in the growing tendency among schools to schedule extracurricular activities on Sunday morning, and in the establishment of Christian schools by those who, in earlier days, strongly advocated the public schools. Rarely do we any longer find major business and civic leaders teaching in our Sunday schools as they did in previous generations.

John Westerhoff has correctly criticized American Protestantism for responding to this situation by expanding the increasingly isolated Sunday school with additional programs and expectations. This response has not filled the void, and I believe that it never will. It is my hope instead, that during the next few years, churches will again discover a way to structure the interdependence of its parts for teaching. Until that happens, however, it is my belief that teachers will be surrounded by institutional confusion, overwhelmed by a sense of isolation, and confronted by the pressure of special-interest groups. To be faithful to the intent of the experience of the community of faith grounded in the traditions of the Bible and the church in this situation will not be easy. To persist in the teaching task will require courage. To ignore the clamor of contending voices for our commitments will be difficult. To expect honor and reward for our efforts will be useless. The isolation of those who accept the responsibility to teach for the community is real and should not be underestimated.

We can no longer assume that the designated teaching roles of a congregation can be filled by just anyone who agrees to teach. For far too long and in far too many places, children, youth, and adults have been hampered by people in teaching roles, especially in the church school, who could not yet articulate their own faith commitments. These students have been "taught" by too many people who have evaluated the teachings of the church by the limits of their own religious experience, who have had little or no sense of the creative flow of the history of the church, and who are still unable to recreate and re-present their understandings and commitments in words and activities that engage students at critical points in their own faith pilgrimages. If teaching is to be taken seriously, a congregation must begin to be increasingly clear about the experience, preparation, and commitments it requires of its teachers. Perhaps one of the most helpful ways this shift could be made would be by changing the content of most teacher-training events, from exercises in pedagogy to experiences designed, first, to help teachers enter into and appropriate their own faith heritage more fully. A second element might entail opportunities for teachers to articulate their own commitments for themselves and finally for those they teach. And the third element might involve identifying in their experience some methods and strategies they could use in communicating what is important to them. These skills may be among the most effective tools in their teaching. In any event, once a congregation has thus taken steps to clarify its teachers' role and faith, teachers may begin to acquire new ways of approaching their teaching task to enhance their effectiveness.

At this point, we may return to a theme struck in the opening pages: in spite of these limitations, teaching is taken seriously by those who have a keen sense of their corporate identity and a deep commitment to the values of their common life for the future. They do not assume that the meaning, values, rituals, and beliefs they now have will be handed on to the next generation in our increasingly fragmented world. Rather, they teach because they believe that the community's originating events still have the power to shape the future. They teach because they keenly sense their responsibility to serve as the link between ancestors and descendents. They teach that people might not be trapped in an eternal present. They teach that the faithfulness of the "saints" of the past might inspire those who will forge the future. They teach so that the resources of the past will not be lost.

Teaching is a crucial function for the survival of any historical community of faith. It is even more important in any community of faith that seeks to be faithful to the intent of its originating events in ever-new situations and circumstances, especially in a social environment were it exists as one community among many. Such is the challenge facing those of us who call ourselves Christian. If we are to be faithful, we must recover the urgency to teach and celebrate the contribution it makes to our common life.

NOTES

Foreword

1. J. Stanley Glen, *The Recovery of the Teaching Ministry* (Philadelphia: The Westminster Press, 1960).

2. *Ibid.*, p. 25.

3. Walter Brueggeman, *Living Toward a Vision: Biblical Reflections on Shalom* (Philadelphia: United Church Press, 1977), p. 30.

4. *Ibid.*

5. *Ibid.*

Chapter 1

1. Brueggeman, p. 15.

2. *Ibid.*

3. John M. Sutcliffe, *Learning Community* (Nutfield, Surrey: Denholm House, 1974), p. 18.

4. Cf. C. F. D. Moule, "Children of God," *The Interpreter's Dictionary of the Bible,* George Buttrick, ed. (Nashville: Abingdon Press, 1962), A–D, pp. 558-61.

5. Urban T. Holmes, III, *Ministry and Imagination* (New York: Seabury Press, 1976), p. 19.

6. Robert McAfee Brown, *Theology in a New Key: Responding to Liberation Themes* (Philadelphia: The Westminster Press, 1978), p. 158.

7. Robert A. Evans, "The Quest for Community," *Union Seminary Quarterly Review,* XXX, 2-4, p. 194.

8. Conrad M. Arensberg and Solon T. Kimball, *Culture and Community* (Gloucester, Mass.: Peter Smith, 1972), p. 1.

9. Evans, p. 194.

10. Louis Joseph Sherrill, *The Gift of Power* (New York: The MacMillan Co., 1961), p. 123.

11. *Ibid.,* p. 125.

12. Evans, pp. 189-90.

13. *Ibid.,* p. 190.

14. *Ibid.*

15. Paul S. Minear, *Horizons of Christian Community* (St. Louis: Bethany Press, 1959), p. 108.

16. Brueggeman, p. 15.

17. Clyde Kluckholn, *Mirror for Man; a survey of human behavior and social attitudes* (Greenwich, Conn.: Fawcett Press, 1944), pp. 42-43.

18. Evans, p. 195.

19. *Ibid.*

20. Ira Progoff, *Jung's Psychology and Its Social Meaning* (New York: Julian, 1953), p. 170.

21. *Ibid.,* p. 66.

22. W. Lloyd Warner, *The Family of God* (New Haven: Yale University Press, 1961), p. 12.

23. Progoff, pp. 67-68.

24. John Steinbeck, *The Winter of Our Discontent* (New York: Bantam Books, 1962; [Viking, 1961]), p. 108.

25. Sidney Earl Mead, *History and Identity* (Missoula, Mont.: Scholars Press, 1979), p. 6.

26. Richard Tholin, "The Holy Spirit and Liberation Movements: The Response of the Church," *The Holy Spirit,* Dow Kirkpatrick, ed. (Nashville: Tidings, 1974), p. 43.

27. Victor W. Turner, *The Ritual Process* (Chicago: Aldine Publishing Co., 1969), p. 96.

28. Frederick Buechner, *The Life of Jesus* (New York: Weathervane Books, 1974), p. 39.

29. Evans, p. 197.

30. *Ibid.,* p. 198.

31. Turner, p. 128.

32. *Ibid.*

33. *Ibid.*

34. *Ibid.*

35. *Ibid.,* p. 113.

36. *Ibid.,* p. 128.

37. Minear, p. 121.

38. *Ibid.*

Chapter 2

1. G. Ernest Wright, *The Biblical Doctrine of Man in Society* (London: SCM Press, 1954), p. 39.

2. Reinhold Niebuhr, *The Nature and Destiny of Man: a Christian Interpretation.* (New York: Charles Scribner's Sons, 1949 [1941]), p. 169.

3. Roland de Vaux, *Ancient Israel; Its Life and Institutions* (New York: McGraw-Hill Book Co., 1961), p. 41.

4. Johns. Pedersen, *Israel; Its Life and Culture* (London: Geoffrey Cumberlege, 1926), p. 101.

5. *Ibid.,* p. 256.

6. David S. Steward and Margaret S. Steward, "Naming into Personhood: The Church's Educational Ministry," *Process and Relationship; Issues in Theory, Philosophy, and Religious Education,* Iris V. Cully and Kendig Brubacher Cully, eds. (Birmingham: Religious Education Press, 1978), p. 50.

7. Pedersen, p. 52.

8. *Ibid.,* p. 53.

9. *Ibid.,* p. 54.

10. Samuel Terrien, *The Power to Bring Forth; Daily Meditations for Lent* (Philadelphia: Fortress Press, 1968), p. 75.

11. *Ibid.,* p. 77.

12. Dennis C. Benson and Stanley J. Stewart, *The Ministry of the Child* (Nashville: Abingdon, 1979), p. 11.

Chapter 3

1. Cf. Edith Turner and Victor Wittar Turner, *Image and Pilgrimage in Christian Culture: Anthropological Perspectives* (New York: Columbia University Press, 1978).

2. John H. Westerhoff III, *Will Our Children Have Faith?* (New York: Seabury Press, 1974).

3. Cf. Robert McAfee Brown, *Is Faith Obsolete?* (Philadelphia: Westminster Press, 1974).

4. Westerhoff, pp. 98-99.

5. Rollo May, *The Courage to Create* (New York: W. W. Norton, 1975), p. 12.

6. Brown, pp. 48-49.

7. *Ibid.,* p. 28.

8. *Ibid.,* p. 32.

9. *Ibid.,* p. 35.

10. *Ibid.,* p. 43.

11. *Ibid.,* p. 44.

12. Brueggeman, p. 54.

13. Brown, pp. 48-49.

14. *Ibid.,* p. 53.

15. Jolande Jacobi, *The Way of Individuation* (New York: Harcourt, Brace and World, 1965), pp. 38-39.

16. *Ibid.,* p. 106.

17. *Ibid.,* p. 97.

18. *Ibid.,* p. 87.

19. *Ibid.,* p. 120.

20. For a thorough discussion of Mark 10:13-16, Luke 18:15-17, and Matt. 18:1-4, see Hans-Reudi Weber, *Jesus and the Children* (Geneva: World Council of Churches, 1979), pp. 22-33. In these passages he explores the problems related to the contexts of the passage in each Gospel, the distinctive use of the phrase, "receive the kingdom," and the metaphorical use of the child in each passage.

21. *Ibid.,* pp. 26-27.

22. *Ibid.,* pp. 28-29.

23. Erik H. Erikson, *Toys and Reasons: Stages in the Ritualization of Experience* (New York: W. W. Norton, 1977), p. 56.

24. Johann Huizinga, *Homo Ludens: A Study of the Play Element in Culture* (Boston: Beacon Press, 1950), p. 4.

25. *Ibid.,* p. 8.

26. *Ibid.*

27. *Ibid.,* p. 9.

28. *Ibid.,* p. 11.

29. Brueggeman, p. 151.

30. *Ibid.*

31. *Ibid.,* p. 161.

32. A statement by Patrick Swazos Hinds, Tesque Pueblo artist posted in the Pueblo Cultural Center, Albequerque, New Mexico, October, 1978. See also Sutcliffe, p. 21.

Chapter 4

1. Maxine Greene, *Teacher as Stranger: Educational Philosophy for the Modern Age* (Belmont, California: Wadsworth Publishing Co., 1973), p. 71.

2. *Ibid.*, p. 175.

3. *Ibid.*, pp. 69-70.

4. Holmes, p. 38.

5. Martin Noth, *The History of Israel* (New York: Harper & Brothers, 1958), p. 333.

6. Paolo Freire, *The Pedagogy of the Oppressed* (New York: Herder and Herder, 1970), pp. 70-71.

7. Greene, p. 69.

8. Brown, p. 33.

9. *Ibid.*, p. 53.

10. Maya Angelou, *I Know Why the Caged Bird Sings* (New York: Random House, 1969).

11. Glen, p. 38.

12. May, p. 20.

13. *Ibid.*, p. 21.

14. *Ibid.*, p. 26.

15. John B. Hough and James K. Duncan, *Teaching: Description and Analysis* (Reading, Mass.: Addison-Wesley, 1970); James Michael Lee, *The Flow of Religious Instruction: A Social Science Approach to Instruction* (Mishawaka: Religious Education Press, 1973).

16. May, p. 30.

17. Margaret Mead, *Culture and Commitment* (Garden City, N.Y.: Doubleday, 1970), p. 17.

18. Locke E. Bowman, Jr., *Teaching Today: The Church's First Ministry* (Philadelphia: The Westminster Press, 1980), p. 90.

19. *Ibid.*

20. Edward T. Hall, *The Silent Language* (Greenwich, Conn.: Fawcett Press, 1959), pp. 69)-70).

21. Jerome Bruner, *Toward a Theory of Instruction* (New York: W. W. Norton, 1960), pp. 40-41.

22. Glenn, pp. 36-37.

23. Maxine Greene, *Landscapes of Learning* (New York: Teachers College Press, 1978), pp. 54-55.

24. *Ibid.*, p. 54.

25. James Smart, *The Strange Silence of the Bible in the Church* (Philadelphia: The Westminster Press, 1970), p. 53.

26. James Sanders, *God Has a Story, Too: Sermons in Context* (Philadelphia: Fortress Press, 1979), p. 8.

27. Charles E. Winquist, *Homecoming: Interpretation, Transformation and Individuation* (Missoula, Mont.: Scholars, 1978), pp. 32 ff.

28. Bowman, p. 94.

29. *Ibid.*, p. 50.